I'D RATHER BE WRIGHT

Other Books by the Authors:

The Future Is Now
William Gildea and Kenneth Turan

Sinema:
American Pornographic Films
and the People Who Make Them
Kenneth Turan and Stephen F. Zito

I'll Always Get Up
Larry Brown with William Gildea

I'D RATHER BE WRIGHT

Memoirs of an Itinerant Tackle

STEVE WRIGHT

with William Gildea and Kenneth Turan

Prentice-Hall, Inc., Englewood Cliffs, N.J.

I'd Rather Be Wright by Steve Wright
with William Gildea and Kenneth Turan
Copyright © 1974 by Steve Wright,
William Gildea, and Kenneth Turan
Printed in the United States of America
Prentice-Hall International, Inc., London
Prentice-Hall of Australia, Pty. Ltd., Sydney
Prentice-Hall of Canada, Ltd., Toronto
Prentice-Hall of India Private Ltd., New Delhi
Prentice-Hall of Japan, Inc., Tokyo

10 9 8 7 6 5 4 3 2 1

Wright, Steve.
   I'd rather be Wright.

   1. Wright, Steve. 2. Football. I. Gildea,
William. II. Turan, Kenneth. III. Title.
GV939.W74A34   796.33'2'0924   74-11168
ISBN 0-13-449785-6

To my parents,
who put up with me
for thirty-two years

FOREWORD

Steve Wright was never all-anything. He seldom was even all-team on his own team. When he played, he usually was an offensive tackle, perhaps the most invisible position in football. Virtually nobody noticed him. But he noticed those around him. And he remembered. But because he was an unimportant player, many people probably will be tempted to dismiss his memoirs as unimportant. They should realize that the memoirs of Steve Wright represent the memoirs of most football players.

Too often only the superstars of sports collaborate on a book. But a superstar's theme invariably is success. Because of his ability, he doesn't understand failure or frustration. And a superstar's experience invariably is limited to one team. Superstars seldom get traded.

Steve Wright was with six National Football League teams and before that he was at the University of

Alabama, which is like being on seven pro teams. I'm just sorry he wasn't with all the NFL teams and at all the big colleges. As it is, he might be unique in that he's been associated with so many of football's famous personalities—the late Vince Lombardi, George Allen, Wellington Mara, George Halas, Paul (Bear) Bryant, Joe Namath, Fran Tarkenton, Sonny Jurgenson, Dick Butkus, Paul Hornung.

His words convey his emotions—his love for Lombardi, for example. Perhaps his link to the glory of the Green Bay Packers in those years spoiled him for other teams but Steve Wright is entitled to at least one happy memory from his frustrating career.

His perspective is personal, almost private. But it should be. It's his book. From it, perhaps the devotees of football will begin to understand that those players whose names are unfamiliar, those players on the bench, those players are people too. Not all these players are capable of expressing their feelings as well as Steve Wright has, but their feelings exist. And their feelings are as important to what football is all about as those of any superstar.

The shame of Steve Wright's career is the shame of other virtually unknown players. Names make news and Steve Wright, like so many others, wasn't a name. So he has remained virtually unknown. At least until now.

In the years when Steve Wright was in New York with the Giants, I never got to know him because I was covering the Jets at the time. But after you read his book, you'll realize, as I did, that it was my loss, not his.

—Dave Anderson

INTRODUCTION

Why Steve Wright?

On first glance, the world is not crying for Steve Wright's book. Even on second and third glances, the same question reappears: Why bother with a 32-year-old offensive tackle who never reached prominence during his thirteen-plus seasons of college and professional football?

More sports books are written every year than most people would care to think about, and almost all share two common denominators. The first is a Big Name: Should a player score enough points, he will probably need a stout mallet to fight off all the potential collaborators who want to tell his story, even if he has no story to tell, which is often the case.

Inevitably, the second common denominator is mind-crushing boredom. Any sportswriter will be happy to tell you that a player's ability to dominate a game is no guarantee of his being a scintillating conversationalist. Reading many of these memoirs means trudging through unending pages of in-depth injury descriptions, copious lists of meals eaten before big games, inspirational talks with one's wife or coach or roommate, sometimes all three, and more. Only 12-year-olds at Christmas can expect to get or enjoy the results.

Steve Wright's story is different. He is a relative unknown who has enormously entertaining things to say. Not many people have heard of him and not all of those who have know he is close to unique among football players because of his wry view of the game.

While talented enough to have played with some of the classic modern teams, Wright is set apart more by his outlook on life and football, a droll detachment which allows him to recognize the ridiculous for what it is. If something is funny, Wright laughs, and this has been interpreted as an anti-football establishment posture that has cost him in terms of salary and prestige.

Yet by a combination of luck and his own ability, no team that Wright has been on has been ordinary. His journey through football has provided him a dryly humorous look at many of the game's leading figures, starting with a national championship team at Alabama quarterbacked by Joe Namath and coached by one of college football's crusty legends, Paul (Bear) Bryant.

His first professional affiliation was with the Green Bay Packers of Vince Lombardi, where he played during the years that team won three NFL championships and two Super Bowls and where he personally gained a certain notoriety as the only player with whom Lombardi lost his temper enough to physically smack.

From Green Bay, Wright went to the New York Giants during two of their most hectic and disorganized years in memory. Cliques, bitter dissension, and general unhappiness were the orders of the day. From the Giants, he moved first to the Sonny Jurgensen/George Allen Washington Redskins, then to the Chicago Bears, ruled by irascible octogenarian George Halas, finally ending it all with the downtrodden St. Louis Cardinals and Philadelphia Eagles.

Steve Wright has not only been in these places, he has remembered what he has seen with his own particular charm, his memory for detail humanizing his recollections. In a sport where yielding to the accepted line sometimes seems as important as winning games, he is hardly the norm. As Larry Merchant of the *New York Post* has written, "Wright has always been somewhat of a misfit in football, not so much because he can't play the game on the field as because he can't play the game off the field. Because he can't hang on every word of the coach as though it is the Grail. Because he doesn't pound his chest like King Kong and breathe fire from his nostrils on the sidelines."

Aggressively independent, Wright has been called a blithe spirit and worse by teams that could not cope with him. Yet his is not the book of a wise guy but that of a recognizable human being who cannot believe what is going on around him. Neither will you.

William Gildea
Kenneth Turan
Washington, D.C.

TABLE OF CONTENTS

Foreword vii

Introduction xi

Alabama 1

Green Bay 43

New York 77

Washington 125

Chicago. . . . . and After 149

I'D RATHER BE WRIGHT

ALABAMA

When I think about the University of Alabama, I spit. They hated my guts down there, and I felt the same about them. We really had a thing for each other. The word on Steve Wright was, "We're going to build his character." Well, I've got news for them: Baby, they really built a character.

It's always been that way with me, people trying to make me different from what I am. I'm 6-foot-6 and 250 pounds now, and I've always been bigger than my peers, so I was expected to do more or to act older than others. You can accept responsibility—and I do—but you can still enjoy yourself at the same time. Because life is enjoyable, it really is. It's fun, I dig it, and I have a good time, and there isn't anyone in the world who can tell me I'm wrong.

Strangely, a lot of people in football don't share this feeling, so my attitude has put me at odds with almost everyone. Even most of the players I've met don't really understand me. They've been taken over by the philosophy preached about the game.

If you're a soldier, you're supposed to kill, if you're a cop, you're supposed to give tickets. Well, football is an emotional sport and I'm a football player, so I'm supposed to be mean. Bullshit.

I'm an easy-going guy. I scare myself when I get mad. Just because I play football doesn't mean I have to go around pushing old ladies and knocking over barstools. You can still be a human being and a man and an individual. I may be big but I'm not an animal, and I don't want to be treated like one.

For about eighteen years, all the way back to high school, football was a very large part of my life. But now, when I watch it on TV, I can't believe that I ever played the game. I sit and watch and I say, You gotta be kidding me. It's really hard for me to believe I did it for all those years. Playing professional football was an experience that's worth a million bucks, but I wouldn't buy it back for fifteen cents. On the other hand, though, I guess I'm a product of everything I've gone through and when I think about the past, all the bullshit and the hospitals and the pain

and the good times and the great times and everything else, I know it wasn't for nothing, because right
now I'm happy with myself the way I am.

Basically, I loved football—the games each week,
that is. It's what goes on in between games, the little
picayune things, that are so annoying. What I don't
like is what some of the owners and coaches have
done to the game. They've taken the enjoyment out
of it. After all, it's a game. I played it hard and I was
good at what I did. With my attitude, I wouldn't have
been around as long as I was if I wasn't good.

Yet in my three varsity years at Alabama I never
started one game. Most of the time they had me with
the injured players, and I wasn't even injured. It was
just ridiculous. They tried to make believe I wasn't
there, but I fooled 'em. I could play football. I knew
it, everyone knew it, but I wasn't playing. All right,
why wasn't I playing?

It comes down to a very hot afternoon in 1961,
my sophomore year. It's like a hundred degrees outside and I was working on a three-on-one reaction
drill. I was on defense. Three offensive men come at
me, and I'm supposed to submarine or drop down to
my knees and stack all of them up neatly in a big pile.

I had gone through it and done it perfectly. I had
done everything I was supposed to do, and I was on
my hands and knees, with my chin strap unbuckled,
trying to get some air, and the assistant head coach, a
guy by the name of Pat James, comes up to me.

"That's pretty good, Wright, except for one thing," he said. "What's that?" I said. Then he just smacked me in the face with a forearm and said, "You're not mean enough." And that was it. He turned around and walked off and there I was holding blood in my hands.

He had split both lips and smashed my nose, and blood just went everywhere. And you're talking about an 18-year-old kid. I had no idea what the hell happened. You talk about a traumatic experience, I'll never forget that. What etched it into my mind more than anything else was the fact that I didn't do anything in reaction. I was too stunned. I guess it damaged my ego as much as anything else, and I just made up my mind right then that there wasn't going to be anyone who pushed me who didn't get pushed back. From that point on it just snowballed. If someone shoved me I'd shove back or if he tried to bust my chops I'd bust his.

Sometimes I'd just laugh because some of the things these supposedly mature and responsible people do are hard to believe. They wouldn't let me start, they tried to kick me off scholarship twice, and I'd laugh at them. When things like that happen I have to laugh. And this is what it comes down to: My sense of humor is what has always gotten me into trouble.

My sense of humor probably came from my parents. They had to be able to laugh because even as a kid I was always getting into trouble. You can just about guess what my middle initial is. I don't even have to go looking for it, trouble always finds me. I don't think my parents had a day go by for fifteen years when there wasn't one phone call that went, "Mrs. Wright, do you have a son named Steve?" The answer was always, "Yeah, what'd he do now?" Because every day something was going on.

I was an All-State defensive tackle at DuPont Manual High School in Louisville, Kentucky, and I had about forty scholarship offers from colleges, mainly because of my size. Most of the schools were in the South and I visited a lot of them.

At Georgia, the guy who was supposed to take me out and entertain me got me a hooker. That impressed me, but then I went down for lunch one time when it must have been 110 degrees outside. The team came in from practice and they had to eat steaming hot chili and I just looked at that chili and I'm saying, No, no, no way.

That trip was surpassed only by one to Tennessee, where the players lived in a dormitory underneath the stadium. It was like a dungeon, plain concrete walls and everything. I went there for lunch once, too, and they had a big plate of bread and a big bowl of gravy. That was it. Uh-uh, that didn't make it either.

One of the coaches who tried to recruit me was Don Doll. Both of us eventually wound up with the Washington Redskins, but at the time he was an

assistant at Notre Dame and he came down to Louisville to talk to me. He came over to the house and was
telling me all about how great Notre Dame was, and the
whole bit, and I said Okay, but you can't have a car
while you're there, isn't that right? He says, Yes, that's
right, and I said, It's an all-male school, and he says yes
again, and I said, Well, what do you do for fun?

He tells me some of the boys catch a bus into
town, and there's always St. Mary's, a girls' school on
the other side of the lake there. Right away I asked
him if I could have a boat—you know, try everything,
you never know unless you ask. He didn't like that
and he said, You understand, we're interested in
serious-minded boys who want to play football. I
said, Boy, have you got the wrong guy.

Eventually I chose Alabama because football at the
time was the greatest thing in the world for me, really
all there was. All of a sudden you're somebody, and
everybody wants to be somebody, and I figured playing at Alabama was my best chance to keep being
somebody.

I was slightly brainwashed at the time because
three of my high school coaches had played for Bear
Bryant when he coached at Kentucky, and they all
said he was the best coach there was. You can get an
education anywhere but if you want to play football
there's only one place to go and that's where Bear
was, at Alabama. So, when they gave me a scholarship, I went.

I'D RATHER BE WRIGHT

I come from an upper middle class family—my father is an engineer for DuPont—where you are taught to do the right thing, respect others, work for your living, get paid for what you do, get a house, raise a family, and do the best you can. So when I went to college I went in with that attitude, like Jesus Christ Superstar, the whole bit. I just wanted to play football. I was going to put everything into it. But I expected to be treated like a human being because that's how I was taught to treat people. I found out it didn't work that way.

Alabama looked like what you'd expect a college to look like, with a quadrangle, the trees, the old buildings. In the spring, they always selected the little Maids of Cotton and had a big blow-out on the lawn in front of the president's mansion—it really was a mansion—and everyone would be decked out in the old Southern costumes, and all the coeds who were chosen queens would parade around with their little bonnets.

Then there was a bell tower called Denny Chimes, a campus landmark, and the whole bit was that whenever a virgin would walk by a brick would fall out, and the thing had been standing for years.

I can remember as a freshman getting up at 5 o'clock in the morning and going over to the practice field, which at the time was right behind the girls' dormitory. You could always tell when somebody got

7

a good look through one of the windows. There might be some chick wanting to show everybody something, and the guys would say, "Hey man, what'd you see?" or "Third window, fourth floor, man, check it out." From there on everyone was trying to find out what room number it was so you could find out the chick's name. This really used to bug Bryant, he'd just start screaming. I couldn't understand why he got so upset. He had the binoculars, we didn't.

Most of the practices were hard, no doubt about it, but they were no different from any other football practices except for the wackos Bryant had for coaches. I never met so many asses in my life as there were on the Alabama coaching staff.

They were all Bryant's robots: When you pushed the button they'd turn this way or that. What do you think about this? Oh yeah. Would you like coffee or tea? Yeah. Yeah, Coach. It was like Bryant was the father, the foster father, and they were his stepchildren, and, Christ, you've got to do anything to please this guy.

Bryant had this tower about forty feet high he used to climb up to watch practice. He'd pick up a megaphone every fifteen or twenty minutes and squawk into it. Nobody could understand what he was saying but, Jesus Christ, you should have seen the coaches go wild. I mean, they'd pick the first kid who was standing next to them and they'd start beating the shit out of him—they didn't know if Bryant was talking to them or not, but just in case he was they sure wanted to be doing something.

The coaches would beat on guys all the time. At Alabama the linemen used to have two-bar face masks and this was the greatest handle in the world. If the coaches wanted to get your attention they'd grab you by the face mask and beat your helmet up and down on your nose, or jerk you around by it. I didn't let too many of them do it, I'd knock their hands away. This didn't endear me either.

Bryant was strictly the general, with his lieutenants doing all the work. He never said much besides hello to me, that was about it. Let's face it, what would he have to talk to me about? For that matter, what'd I have to talk to him about? About the most he ever said to me was, "You better wipe that smile off your face or I'll send you back to Louisville right now." I'd get that pretty often.

Physically, Bryant was a fair-sized man. The story goes that he got the name Bear by wrestling one in a circus sideshow in Arkansas. Anyway, he must have had something because there was one practice when it rained so hard you couldn't see across the parking lot where we had our cars, but not a drop fell on the practice field. It happened, I was there.

He was scared of lightning though, because that tower of his had a metal frame. That was the only thing that could make him call off practice. It could rain like a bitch and nothing would happen, but if lightning started he'd scoot right off of that tower.

Bryant's an impressive person until you know him, especially if you're a high school kid, because he's a very slow and deliberate talker, very convincing. But the more I knew him the less I liked him.

The first time I met him was when I was flown down to Alabama in a private plane with two other football players. As a kid this impresses you, and then you go out on a yacht and they take you to all the places and introduce you to all the right people and the whole bit. It's strictly a snow job.

But when we went over to Bryant's house the first impression I got was that he must be a real egotist because the whole place was covered with nothing but pictures of him. I mean, the basement didn't have two square inches of wall space that was without its picture of Bryant. It made me laugh. I was surprised there weren't just plain wall mirrors instead. It would have saved a lot of trouble.

Bryant was always giving speeches to the freshmen, writing a bunch of stuff up on the blackboard and talking about character and discipline and using, or at least trying to use, all kinds of big words. Once he said, "Remember, when you're an Alabama football player you're with the e-light." I'm thinking, what the hell's "e-light," and he keeps saying it, how Alabama is and stands for the e-light. I thought he must be talking about the Statue of Liberty with her light, or something, I'm trying to figure this out, and all of a sudden it dawned on me he's saying "elite" and he doesn't know how to pronounce it.

And you can bet nobody said, "Oh, do you mean 'elite?' " 'Cause that kid was gone right then.

By the time I graduated, Alabama had a fancy athletic dormitory, but in my freshman year we lived in an old dilapidated place called Friedman Hall, which had a meeting room downstairs where Bryant would give these talks. One day he started by telling us that the paramount thing was to get an education but not to forget that we were also there to play football. About this time, the doors behind him started shaking and he looked at them like, Stop! doors, if you don't I'm gonna kill you, like he had some kind of power over inanimate objects.

He started to talk to us again and the door started shaking again and he turned around, kicked it wide open, and just started screaming. There was nobody there for him to scream at, but he's screaming anyway. And you're just sitting there and you're saying to yourself like, there's gotta be somebody there, because nobody screams at thin air, right? No, uh-uh, nobody there. It was really something. It was like a piece of theater, he probably just wanted to let us know he could scream.

I got another little insight into Bryant when I was a junior and we played Vanderbilt. We were supposed to just annihilate them and we only beat them 17-7, and that really pissed Bryant off so he called a meeting for Sunday, the next day, at 5 o'clock in the morning.

Bryant comes in and starts going over what was wrong with the game, and the main thing he says was that everybody was arm-tackling. And he gives a demonstration of how to do things right, how you gotta flex your knees and get in the football position and tackle with your shoulder and your head, the whole bit.

Then he calls up one of his assistant coaches, a kid by the name of Charlie Pell, later the head coach at Jacksonville State, who had graduated the year before. Charlie gets up and he stands in front of Bryant and Bryant goes to tackle him and knocks him over about three chairs. Everybody kind of snickers and Bryant says, Well, no, that's not really what I mean, come back here and we'll do it again.

So Charlie says, Duh, okay Coach, dusts himself off, straightens the chairs out and goes back and stands in front of Bryant again and sure enough, bam, Bryant hits him again and knocks him over three more chairs.

By this time you can tell there's something amiss somewhere. Like the first time could be an accident, the second time, uh-uh. Then he calls him back a third time, and with this Charlie is a little hep to the situation and Bryant only knocks him back a couple of feet.

It turns out that Charlie was ten minutes late for the coaches' 4 a.m. meeting and all this was simply Bryant's way of slapping his wrist.

Bryant seemed to enjoy the role of disciplinarian, and he got plenty of opportunity to perform. The football team he recruited was about 80 percent farm boys—some never even had shoes until they got to the University, they'd as soon sit on a nail keg as a nice chair. Whenever they were unsupervised in the dorm they'd just tear the place apart, throwing beer bottles down the hall, tossing chairs back and forth from one room to another. The place could have been a shambles in two days unless these guys were disciplined.

So Bryant kept trying to make gentlemen out of them, especially after the University put up a new athletic dorm named after him my last season there. It's a beauty, no doubt about it, really a posh facility. It's got four or five big double doors, and in the entrance room there's a big fireplace with a huge copper hood. Everything's in red and white, Alabama's colors. It has plush, red carpets and white chairs and a big white rug in front of the fireplace. But the whole thing was, You don't touch this and you don't walk on that and only on weekends when you have the family in can you sit down anywhere.

Sometimes Bryant overdid the discipline. The TV room was the pride of the place and Bryant had made an announcement that since we are all going to be gentlemen, whenever an adult walks into a room you rise because this is what all young gentlemen do.

One night there're about three of four of us sitting in this room watching television and Bryant walks in and looks at us. We say, How're you doing, Coach, and he just looks around and walks back out. About five seconds later he comes walking back in, goes over to the television, turns it off, and says, I told you you're supposed to stand when an adult walks into a room. Well, I'm an adult and I didn't see anybody stand, so we're gonna practice some etiquette.

With this he walked out of the room and we sat down, he walked into the room and we stood up, he walked out of the room and we sat down, he walked back into the room and we stood up again. And then, just to let us know that he was still really pissed off at us, he wouldn't let us watch any more television.

So this is Bear Bryant for you.

Not that his assistants were any better. Pat James, the guy who smacked me in the face, used to give his little talks, too. One day we're sitting out on the field and he's telling us how we ought to block on a plane, that Coach Bryant wants you to block on a plane, now do it just like you're gonna take off like an airplane.

And I'm saying, Uh, Coach, I don't think that's what he meant when he said block on a plane. Right then I knew I should've kept my big mouth shut again because he just looks and says, "Who's coaching, me or you?" You know it ain't ever gonna be me.

James had a brother who I think was killed in the Second World War and that was all he could talk about. "You guys are the ones I want to go to war with," he'd say. "We gotta go out there and kill those Japs."

It was really weird the way you could see this building up in him before a game. His face would turn red, he'd get up in front of everyone like he was going to lead a Bonzai charge himself and he'd scream, "We gotta go out there and we gotta kill them Japs." And I'm looking at him and I'm thinking, You've got to be kidding me. I'm going out there to play a football game, man.

I got back at James once, even though it was an accident. We had been out on the field for a long time. It was dark, we couldn't see, and he had been chewing me out for one thing or another all day and again I just laughed. The hell with it, I could've cared less, and then a typical thing happened, because I don't have to go looking for trouble, I'm like a magnet, it just naturally adheres to me.

We were working on a punt block drill. At that time the rules were if you blocked a punt you could just keep batting the ball downfield as you're trying to pick it up. Once, we even made a touchdown by doing that.

So we had two guys rushing the punter and we had

15

to block the ball and then chase and kick it down-field, even though it was so dark you could hardly see the punter or the football or anything else. I was kicking a ball downfield, about thirty or forty yards. Finally I fell on it and started bringing it back. When I got a little closer I said, Here you go Coach, and threw the ball and—you know what's gonna happen—it hit him right in the head.

You never saw so many football players just vacate an area so fast. James whips around and it's like, Who's there? And all he can see is this big shadow, and nobody had to ask who that was. What are you gonna do?

One of the worst coaches at Alabama was Charlie Bradshaw, at one time the infamous Kentucky coach who ran everyone out and almost ended up without enough players for a team. He's probably the biggest hypocrite I ever met in my life. College coaches have got to be the greatest liars in the world. They're worse than used car salesmen, they really are. They're all two-faced, back-stabbing sons of bitches, and they wouldn't think twice about screwing you.

When you're a kid they come down and tell you, Boy, you're probably one of the greatest high school athletes in the world. We want you to come down here with us. It's like a political campaign speech, Come down and I'm gonna give you everything, boy. Now all you gotta do is sign on the line and I'll give you everything. Well, forget it.

We used to call Bradshaw Silver Tongue because off the field he was the straight Southern Baptist. Everything was Christian, like That's a great Christian car you got there, man, wow, I bet Jesus would really love that.

He'd tell everyone how he wanted good Christian boys from good Christian families to play at this good Christian school in the great Christian game of football. You kept waiting to see a silver chalice or something out there when you walked on the field.

But when Bradshaw got on the field, Christ, he became an animal. I've seen him just beat the shit out of kids. One of his little tricks was when he saw somebody doing something wrong he would start off at a slow trot from about fifteen or twenty yards back and increase his speed until he got to within about a yard of the player and just fly through the air and hit him in the face with a forearm. If a coach ever tried that in the pros, they'd kill him, he wouldn't walk off the football field.

And again, you're talking about 18 or 19-year-old kids who had to play football or there was no way they were going to get to college. So they had to take this.

Bradshaw had another interesting habit. It would get 100-105 degrees in the summer and Bucky—we also called him Bucky—used to do one of those things that really bugs you.

He'd come up and start chewing you out about

17

three inches from your face. Getting chewed out wouldn't bother me, but he used to really foam at the mouth, too. You'd get just covered with spit while you're getting chewed out and you gotta stand there and take it. That's really demoralizing. There was always a great temptation to hawk it right at him, to blow one right back in his face.

At least, after I left Alabama, those coaches never forgot about me. When I was playing for Green Bay we had a prospect come up to one of our games from Texas A&M, where Gene Stallings, an old Alabama assistant, was the head coach.

I started talking to him and said, Oh, you went to Texas A&M, and he says, Yeah. I said, You gotta know Beebs pretty good then—Beebs is Stallings' nickname—and he says Yeah again. Then I told him how I'd had a lot of fun with old Beebs, he was my coach at Alabama.

All of a sudden the kid gets all excited and says, Oh, you're the one, and I said, Yeah, I'm the one. Jesus, he says, I was talking to Coach Stallings before I left and he said you're the worst football player he ever coached in his life. I said I kinda felt the same way about him as a coach.

Eventually, I realized that these people who are supposedly molding the character of our youth are unable to communicate with anybody except on a basic animalistic level. They can't make it any other way. They have no concept of what goes on in the world. They live in their own little sphere of influence, which is football, and they can get away with whatever they want to. They're not educators, they're shallow people, they don't care about you. So I just said fuck 'em.

Despite all the trouble I eventually got into, when I started out as a freshman everyone had high hopes for me because I wouldn't take any shit from the varsity players. I felt, Okay, so I'm a freshman but just because you're a sophomore or a junior or a senior doesn't mean you can come over and push me around or tell me what to do or anything else. That was an attitude the coaches liked.

I got into three or four fights and, again, this was good as far as the coaches were concerned. I'd take just so much but I wasn't going to take a heck of a lot. One time I was playing defense and a kid by the name of Mike Fracchia, some star fullback, came running across to block me and I just knocked him on the ground. Freshmen aren't supposed to do that, so he got mad and kicked at me with his foot. Then they ran the same play again and he tried to kick me again and we just went at it right there on the spot.

We couldn't really hurt each other because we had our face masks and everything else on, and I sure wasn't going to take mine off. One time I saw a freshman and a senior get into a fight and the coaches kept screaming, Let 'em fight it out but make 'em take their helmets off, they're gonna break their hands. And the stupid freshman took his helmet off and the senior beat the shit out of him. So you learn fast.

After it was over the coaches all come over to you and it's like, That's the way, yeah, don't take anything off of them, you're gonna be good, and all this stuff. They liked the attitude at first, but they had never experienced it to the degree I had it. I mean, I wouldn't take anything from them, either. And they'd always been able to break everybody else.

They started working on me the summer after my freshman year. My grades hadn't been too good, so the coaches told me to go to summer school, just show up and not worry about a thing. I checked into the dormitory and went to Carney Laslie, the assistant athletic director, to get my food money. Laslie was Bryant's whipping boy. Anything that was wrong was Carney's fault. You know, if it rained, man, he was in trouble.

Well, Carney says to me, No, your name's not on the list, you better go see Coach Bryant. So I went into Bryant's office and told him I had been told I was going to be on scholarship for summer school.

Hell no, he says, you almost flunked out, we don't want people like you. If you can't do it by yourself we're sure as hell not going to do anything for you. And this was after the assistant coaches had told me everything would be taken care of.

The idea was strictly to make me beg for my

scholarship. Let's build his character, and let's make him eat a little shit to help build him up. They wanted to make me more humble because I was too quote, unquote, cocky, and they didn't like that. They wanted someone who was going to crawl and beg, but that just ain't Steve Wright.

So I called my dad, and luckily my dad is not stupid. He came up to see Bryant and showed him the agreement I'd signed with Alabama and told him, It's got your name on it and his name on it and it says nothing about grades being a criterion for a scholarship. So they paid for my books and my tuition, everything but food. I didn't eat too well that summer.

Things definitely didn't improve after that. It didn't take a whole lot for me to get on somebody's shit list. They tried the scholarship bit again my junior year, and my father had to come down with the same paper. I knew I couldn't afford to step out of line, because if they ever had a chance to screw me they would. And whenever they'd try, I'd tell 'em, Uh-uh, almost, but you didn't get me. And, of course, that irritated them. I'd stick it right in their ear. I'd say, Yeah, I know you're trying to get rid of me but you ain't gonna do it, baby.

One of the most insidious things they did was change my roommate. All of a sudden one day a coach comes up and says, Wright, you move in with this other fellow, and this other fellow turns out to be the biggest pig you ever saw in your life.

I mean nobody would even touch this kid. The trainer wouldn't even let him come in the training room. He wouldn't touch him because the kid never took a shower. He was living by himself in the dormitory and he chewed tobacco and he'd spit the juice out the window on the other side of the room and sometimes he'd make it and sometimes he wouldn't.

So I bought a bottle of Lysol and cleaned up my side of the room and I got him one of those big vegetable cans and put it by his bed and I said, All right, this is yours. I don't ever want to see a piece of tobacco or anything else on that side of the room. I was bigger than he was so he listened.

Another time they put me in with a guy who did nothing but read comic books. I never saw so many comic books in my life, just stacks and stacks of them. That's all the kid ever read. He'd come back from classes, throw his books down, pick up a comic book, and that was it. Unbelievable. Comic books—that was his whole existence.

On the field, I was singled out constantly. The favorite word at Alabama was turd, and I got called that so many times that when I heard it I kind of automatically said, Yeah, what do you want?

Just about every day some coach would come up to me and say, You're no good, you can't be a ball player and all of this bullshit and then talk to some of the other players like, If you can't beat this turd you're not worth a damn either.

This sort of thing reached a peak my senior year while we were practicing for my last game, the Sugar Bowl against Mississippi. It was some line drill and all of a sudden Bryant comes up to a guy across from me and starts shaking him around by the face mask saying, "You, you're the reason Wright's never been any good, people like you, you don't make him work hard enough, that's the trouble with him, he could be the greatest football player in the world, but people like you won't make him work."

Meanwhile, I'm just standing there looking at this like, What are you doing, huh, get out of here. And so then he turns to me and grabs my face mask, but I tense up and he can't move me. And I've got this grin all over my face, I'm just looking him right in the eye like, Get outa here, go play with the hogs or something.

After he sees he isn't going to be able to budge me, he gives me some line like, Get back in the huddle and play like you're supposed to play. So I walk back to the huddle and I'm laughing by this time, I'm just cracking up, and the huddle, the huddle starts to move away.

If you can imagine ten guys actually moving away and here I am trying to catch up to them. "Wait for me guys," I'm saying, "Hey, wait for me." And Bryant is shouting, "Wipe that grin off your face or

I'll send you home right now." And I just turned to him and gave him another look like, That's fine with me, baby.

There were all kinds of physical punishment, too. The coaches would invariably have the lower teams make up for the mistakes of the first two, so the third and fourth teams would have to just beat the shit out of each other all day—nothing but butting heads—and the coaches would jump up and down and scream, the whole bit.

Then there was what they called the board drill. A board was put on the ground, it was about ten feet long and twelve inches wide, and they made one man stand at one end while the whole team would take turns trying to knock him off. You'd stand up there for a while and the first guy'd run down the board at you and you'd knock him down and the second guy'd come and you'd knock him down, and after a while you'd realize, Hey, I'm getting the shit beat out of me. I'm beating all the people but nobody's taking my place, I'm just standing here and getting it. So after a while you'd manage to get knocked down yourself and then you could go to the end of the line and rest.

There was even stuff to do before spring practice started. They had a conditioning program that was compulsory for all football players to attend. It amounted to forty-five minutes of intense physical activity, the worst part taking place on wrestling mats.

24

What this amounted to was just putting everybody on the mats and having them try to knock everybody else off. And the last guy left wins. So you do this for fifteen minutes straight, just beat the shit out of each other, with the coaches standing there yelling, Go Go, and all that. I finally decided, screw this, it was illegal to have us out before spring practice anyway, and I told them I wasn't coming anymore.

As a form of punishment for that they would make me get up at 5 o'clock in the morning and one of the coaches would come out and I'd run around the track until he decided I'd run enough. So I decided if I wasn't playing football I might as well start getting an education, so I devoted that semester, the second of my junior year, to improving my grades. I studied. I'd stay up all night studying. And the greatest thing was that I knew the coach, who turned out to be my old buddy Pat James, wasn't up all night like I was, he had to get up special at 4:30 to come out with me at 5. I'd meet him over at the track and he'd just say, Okay, go out there and start running. I'd set a pace for myself and go over in my mind all the notes I'd made during the night. And that was the way I studied.

Another thing was the wave drill. You'd get in a football stance, picking your feet up and down, taking choppy steps, and going in the direction of the coach's hands, either right or left or backward or forward.

I was 6-6 and 240, but the coach kept saying, Wright, you gotta get lower, get lower, and like I'm getting down lower and I'm getting down lower and all of a sudden I'm squatting and I'm not doing anything but moving my arms. And he keeps saying, Get lower, get lower, and I'm saying, Christ, what do ya want me to do, sit on the floor?

Then he says, Stop, everybody stop. Get out here in front, Wright, I want you to do it, I'll make you get down. So here I am, 6-6, I'm squatted so far down that I can't pick up my feet off the ground, all I'm doing is swinging my arms and that's it, and he's still going, You gotta get lower, you gotta get lower. And I'm saying You're outa your mind, I can't get any lower.

So with that this jerkoff goes over and picks up a big strap that was used to tie up the mats after we were finished, and he starts hitting me with it, like I'm some Roman galley slave, and he's screaming, Get lower, get lower, and it's like there's no way, I can't pick up my feet, I can't walk, I can't even move.

So I just resorted to the old Steve Wright, I fell over on my back and started cracking up laughing at this guy. He was standing there beating me with this strap and I was laughing at him like, What are you doing, anyway? He stopped pretty soon because he saw I was making a fool of him. Maybe now you can see why I got into some trouble down there.

Because of all this I wasn't exactly the most popular guy on the Alabama team. It got to be pretty common knowledge not to mess with me, that I was always getting into trouble. Sometimes players would come up and say they wished they had the guts to do what I was doing, but more often it was, You gotta be out of your mind to do that, what do you mean you're not gonna go to the gym, you're gonna be in trouble. I'd tell them, How can I be in trouble, it's against the rules, if they wanna bust me, I'll bust them. That attitude didn't go over too well at all.

The only player I got along with was a guy named Joe Sisia. We got together because of our interest in hunting, but Joe soon got in the same category I was because he was an Italian from New Jersey, an automatic Yankee, and he didn't let 'em forget it. Like he knew who won the war, too. And on top of that he drove a Cadillac, it was only a 1953, but it was a Cadillac, and this used to bug the coaches. They were only driving Fords, and it was always Sisia and that goddamn Cadillac.

The coaches knew Joe and I were friends so they would punish us by putting us together in one-on-one drills and have us beat on one another. Both of us knew when it was coming because the coaches would sit there saying, You and you go at it, and all of a sudden Joe's looking at me and I'm looking at him and sure enough they've got us together again.

Joe used to go out of his way to antagonize the

coaches. He smoked, and Alabama's philosophy about that was, Now we don't want you to smoke but we know some of you do, so if you're gonna smoke just do it in your rooms. But once a month they would check your rooms and if they caught you smoking you had to get up at 5 o'clock the next morning and run the stadium steps, so there was no way you could win. But Joe, Joe was all over the campus with a cigarette in his mouth, when we'd go to eat, when he was driving his car, the whole time.

He was no different on the field. Charlie Bradshaw hit him once and he chased Bradshaw all over the place. Bryant even made one of his rare trips down from his tower, walked over to Joe and said, Boy, that's what I like to see JoJo, you really got enthusiasm, you really get excited, that's what we need around here.

But it was just the opposite. Joe was gone, gone because he was somebody who wouldn't take the shit they were handing out. So they found a way to kick him off scholarship. I think he and maybe fifteen other players had copied somebody's term paper from two or three semesters back, but Joe was the only one who got kicked off scholarship.

And the incredible part was that after they had sent him a letter telling him they didn't want his kind of football player playing for Alabama, that he was a disgrace and everything, one of the coaches told him he was expected to come back out for the team.

Again, they want you to come beg them for a chance.

There was only one way you could get away with the stuff Sisia tried—and that was if your name was Joe Namath. He was a year behind me and he was the biggie, he was Bryant's boy.

Bryant always had his arm around him, going to practice, walking off the field, or whatever. Joe was in a different category. He did what he wanted to do and got away with it because of his football ability. Being a star lets you get away with things nobody else can.

Joe had this whole entourage, they would drive all over campus drinking and carrying on. The chauffeur was a guy named Hootowl Hicks, and it was like he'd lay down in a puddle for Joe to walk over. He was the equipment manager, he'd hand out the jerseys and things. Joe used to put him through his paces: sit up, roll over, play dead.

There was another guy with them who had to be the skinniest kid in the world. I think he was about 5-7 and maybe a hundred pounds, and I couldn't figure that out. He had to be missing something, he couldn't have everything inside I got inside, you know something's got to be missing somewhere.

He used to do some dance, I don't know what the hell it was, the Alabama Shuffle or whatever, but it used to crack Joe up, so it was always, Lemme see ya dance. It might be in the middle of the dining hall or out in front of a classroom, all Joe'd have to do was say, Lemme see ya dance, and this dude would start shuffling away.

Even as a prospect, Joe was cocky. The first day he came down to look at the campus, he went up Bryant's tower. Nobody goes up that tower but Bryant, it was unheard of, nobody else ever went up in the four years I was there. Apparently Bryant said something to Joe like, Do you think you can climb up there? And he said, Yeah, and up he went. No one could believe it, all the players wanted to know, Who's that jerk up there with the coach? But Joe didn't worry, he always knew he had it made.

Joe copied his style at Alabama from Ray Abbruzzese, who later ended up with him on the Jets. Ray is typical dark-haired, good-looking guy, do anything for you, heck of a nice guy.

When Joe first got to the campus he was nothing but a high school kid, and because Ray was from Philadelphia and Joe was from Pennsylvania, they just kinda came together. And after a while you could see where Joe would kinda talk like Ray or use the same lines. After Ray went with the Buffalo Bills, the AFL paid him to come down to Alabama and persuade Joe to go with New York. So he just lived on campus with Joe for about six months, and then when Joe went to the Jets Ray went with him and they were roommates in New York.

My friend Joe Sisia once told me he thought I was probably the beginning of the downfall of Bryant as the absolute disciplinarian, and that Namath finished him off. I don't know about that but I'd say this about Bryant and me: All of a sudden he found someone who didn't think he was God, who looked at him as normal—well, no, he certainly wasn't normal—who looked at him as a man, like everyone else. Everyone was scared of him and I haven't met anybody yet I'm scared of. Bryant had tremendous power, he'd say shit and you'd ask where. Well, most people would. I never did, and that's what got me in trouble.

Maybe just the years have mellowed Bryant some. Again, though, I just might have been the first player he'd had who viewed things the way kids do today. Wait a minute, what do you mean run my head into the wall, for what? You tell me to do something constructive that I'm gonna benefit from and yeah, but run my head into the wall? Does my neck need strengthening, or what?

This is what the kids that I went to school with didn't have. Bryant would tell you to run until you dropped, just because he's telling you to, and they would. If Coach Bryant tells me to run my head into the wall, I'm gonna run my head into the wall, because if I don't then I'm off scholarship. That's the way it was.

I don't think I really realized until my junior year that Alabama was never going to start me in a game. I kept trying to make it. I kept figuring they can't be that stupid, but I was wrong, wrong again. I knew I was a good football player, and I figured how could you not play somebody who wants to play, somebody who can play well. But you bet they found a way, and they didn't have to work too hard at it either.

As a sophomore, it was really frustrating. You keep thinking you're gonna work your way up and you ask yourself and everyone else, What am I doing wrong, what can I do? And it was, You gotta do this, you gotta get lower, you gotta get meaner, you gotta do fifteen million different things and I said okay. So you go out there and you do it and nothing happens, you never make it above the third team. And again you have to realize that as a kid this was my first real encounter with something like this, being shut out completely. I really didn't know how to handle it. It seemed like there wasn't anything I could do right except for one thing and that was to be me.

I never got as high as the second team, which means I never got into an Alabama game, until the last six games of my senior year. There were five teams, and then the injured players, and where I was depended on the mood of the day, like, Where're we gonna put him today? Each team had a color. The red team was the first team, the white team was the second team, the blue team was the third, the green team was the fourth, and the orange was the fifth. Then there was the yellow team, the injured players.

32

They'd put me there most of the time whether I was hurt or not. They just loved giving me that yellow jersey.

Bryant had a challenge system. If you thought you were better than someone ahead of you at your position you had the right to challenge him. So I told my friend Pat James, the guy who hit me, that I'd like to challenge the starting tackle, a kid by the name of Steve Allen.

He said to talk to Coach Bryant, and Bryant said, Well, all right, we'll do it tomorrow. Okay. So tomorrow came, and we started pre-practice warm-ups, and nothing happened. We started practice and nothing happened. We went all the way through practice, the first team went in, then the second team, and still nothing happened. So I walked over to Bryant and told him I thought he was going to let me challenge Steve Allen.

Bryant said, Oh yeah, I forgot about that. Well, there's the third team tackle, go challenge him. I said, Bullshit, if I'm gonna challenge someone I want to go right to the top, to the first guy, what the hell do I want to challenge the third team tackle for? He says, Well, you just can't do it. And I said, Well, just screw it, and I walked off the field and that was it. The whole thing was, I knew I could beat Steve Allen, Steve Allen knew I could beat Steve Allen, everybody else knew I could beat Steve Allen, but there was no way it was going to happen.

There were other disadvantages to being on the shit list, and I mean all the way at the bottom of it. Everyone on the whole football team was supposed to get at least two tickets to all home games. My folks came to every game and all of a sudden before one of them two people on the whole football team didn't get their two tickets, and you know who one of them was. I ended up paying one of the other players sixty dollars for two of his tickets.

My parents understood what was going on and my mother even decided that I needed something to occupy my time while I was sitting on the bench, so she bought me one of those big executive Yo-Yos. You better believe I toyed with the idea of using it. I used to kid with people, saying I was going to bring it along. I even packed it in my bag one time, but I just didn't have enough guts to use it. I was walking a thin line all the way, and I knew the first chance the coaches had off I'd go, and using that Yo-Yo would have been my big mistake. I would have made my attitude perfectly clear to about 40,000 people.

Then, just before our game with Mississippi State my senior year, they put a list up on on the wall and all of a sudden there I was on the second team. Oh boy, oh boy, oh boy, I get to play, I get to play! Hey guys, look at this, second team, wow, man, I got me a white jersey.

The reason I got to play was that the coaches knew

the pros were interested in me, there were pro scouts down looking at me all the time. If I made it with the pros and never played football at all at Alabama, how would it look? The great Bear Bryant and he never played me? So they decided to let me in.

But there was some concern that since I'd never played when I did get in a game I might look bad and embarrass Alabama. So they provided me with my own personal coach, Dude Hennessey. My own private coach!

I already knew Dude, he had been with me a little bit in high school, and he was one of the guys who brainwashed me about Alabama. Also, his wife had lived right next door to a girl I was dating in Louisville, so I knew him pretty well. I think he had nothing else to do at Alabama, he was just there, they had to find something for him to do, so they made him my coach. Hell, he's only about 5-6, but he was supposed to take me under his wing. So every day, once practice started, me and Dude would go off in a corner somewhere.

It was a fun time because I was 6-6, and the biggest player Bryant had ever had at tackle might have been 6-2 and 180 pounds. Now he's playing me at that position, and it just doesn't work. There's no way I'm gonna get down as low as a smaller guy. So they put me at defensive end, more of a stand-up job, and every day Dude did nothing except tell me to go out there and bite 'em and scratch 'em and so on. It was really a joke. I never did start, but I played long enough to earn my one and only Alabama letter.

A friend of mine wrote to Alabama recently asking about me and they told him I'd lettered twice. Now I didn't know that, I'll be doggone if you don't learn something new every day. It's that goddamn publicity department again. They must have a heck of a PR man, I'll tell you. Wait till this book comes out, I'll be listed as All-American.

I really don't know how the pros found out about me. I guess they'd seen me at practice. I was the biggest guy there, and I was always there, I was out there longer than anybody. I worked hard at practices because I knew the coaches were trying to run me off the team and I wouldn't let them have the satisfaction of succeeding. I wasn't too confident of getting drafted, but I guessed I might. I'd answered a couple of questionnaires from the Dallas Cowboys and the Los Angeles Rams but I never heard from them again. If I wasn't drafted by the pros I thought about going into the Marines to avoid the other draft. I would've had a tremendous attitude there, wouldn't I? They would've loved me.

But the pro draft turned out to be beautiful. I had a clock radio and it went on all of a sudden one morning to wake me up for an 8 o'clock class and I heard on the news that I had been drafted fifth by the Green Bay Packers and seventh by the New York

Jets, two teams I'd never heard a word from. That was pretty incredible for the amount of time I'd played, so I figured, screw it, I'll celebrate a little bit. So I turned the radio off, went back to sleep, and cut all my classes for the day.

When the draft choices became known, all the coaches at Alabama began pushing for Green Bay like a bitch. You don't want to go with the Jets, boy, nah, you'll hate it up there. But that Green Bay, man, that's the greatest team in the world, boy, it's fantastic, I wish I could play for them. To a man it was Green Bay, Green Bay, Green Bay, like they were getting paid off or something. It was really ridiculous to see these guys fall all over themselves, and all over me, after I'd been in the doghouse for more than two years. Dig it, this is what I'm laughing at, who are you guys trying to kid?

If I'd had to choose between the two teams on the basis of initial meetings, I probably would have gone with the Jets. We were at Mobile, getting ready for the Sugar Bowl game with Mississippi, and somehow I'd gotten food poisoning, I'm sick as a dog. I'm running off the field like crazy, man, I can't even move without a cork.

So I'm recuperating in my hotel room and I get a call from George Sauer, Sr., of the Jets. He was in the hotel across the street so I went over and he answered all my questions right down the line, no trouble at all.

Getting to see someone from Green Bay was

something else. The next day at practice my old buddy Dude Hennessey tells me, There's a coach here from Green Bay but I don't think you should see him before the game because Bryant might get mad. I said, Screw him, this is between me and the Packers, it's got nothing to do with Bryant. If he wants to see me tell him to come see me, or, if you want, I'll go see Bryant myself and tell him what I'm going to do.

That day as I was leaving dinner this coach comes up and introduces himself as Red Cochran from the Packers and says, I'd like to talk to you but the coaches don't think it would be a good idea before the game. I said, That's bullshit because I want to see you, there're some questions I want answered, and I'm going to call Bryant right now and tell him. Fine, says Cochran, and I go back to my room to call.

I'm not there more than fifteen seconds when the phone rings. It's Cochran, and he says, I'll tell you what. I talked with the coaches and they really don't think it's a good idea to bother Bryant so I'll just come up to your room in fifteen minutes, and I said, Fine.

In less than five minutes, the phone rings again, and this time it was Dude Hennessey. He says his wife, the woman I knew from Louisville, was downstairs and wanted to see me. I told him I was waiting for Cochran, and he says, That's all right, you'll be back in plenty of time, come on down, and so I said okay again.

38

I walk down the stairs and I see Dude but I don't see his wife anywhere. He says, Oh, she's back here, come with me, and we walk back to some corner behind the phone booths and everything else and he says, Look, my wife's not here, I talked it out with Red Cochran and we decided it would be better if no one knew about this meeting at all. So he's going to meet you across the street in the parking lot. And that was to be my first experience with the fabled Green Bay Packers, trying to find some coach in a parking lot.

I went over to the lot and it was really beautiful. I'm looking around through all the cars and everything else, I'm searching the dude out, yelling, Hey Red, where are you, man? Here boy, here Red. Finally he peeks out from inside some car and kind of whispers, Hey, back here.

We drove over to his hotel but once we got there, after all this nonsense, I found the guy didn't know a thing, or at least he pretended not to. I wanted to find out about salary and the type of contract they had and things like that and I don't think he answered one question straight. It was all bullshit about, Well, but this is the Green Bay Packers. I said, Yeah, I know, but what if this happens or that happens and all I got is a tape recording. This is the Green Bay Packers, This is the Green Bay Packers, This is the Green Bay Packers. Not too impressive.

Unfortunately for the Jets, though, they switched

from Sauer to another coach. I had seen enough of his type, the backdoor, two-faced, hypocritical sons of bitches, at Alabama, and I spotted another one right off. He tried to push me into signing with the Jets. Let's sign now, he'd say. It was always, Sign now, we won't tell anyone until after the game. That so irritated me I made a tentative agreement with the Packers to sign for one year for $12,000 plus a $9,000 bonus—remember, this was a year before Joe Namath and the big stuff. And I signed in the locker room after the Sugar Bowl game.

When I told this guy at the Jets what I was going to do, he asked? How much did you agree to sign for, and I said it didn't make any difference. Then he produces this signed blank check, there weren't any figures on it at all, and I'm thinking in a lot of zeros, and he's saying, Just fill it in. Finally I told him I was going with the Packers anyway and he asks me, Well, you didn't already sign with them, did you? and I said no. So he wants to know why I won't tell him how much I agreed to, and I said, Well, mainly because it's none of your business. He wanted to know how he could make a counter-offer, and I told him he couldn't, I just wanted to play for the Packers. Then he says, I'll tell you one thing, when you get to the pros, a lot of us move around and one of these days I'll probably be running across you again, and if I find out that you lied to me, that you've already signed, I'll make it my business to make it tough on you.

That did it. As soon as he said that I just said Fuck you and turned around and walked out the door.

So I really didn't choose Green Bay for the money. It was more personal pride. I didn't know if I could make it in the pros or not, but I knew I was gonna give it a hell of a shot and if I was gonna give it a hell of a shot I might as well go with the best, and that's what the Packers were.

Not really playing for more than two years, being out of the routine of doing something, it makes you wonder. I had something to prove to myself and to a lot of other people. Sure, I could go out there and butt heads with somebody, but as far as playing and really getting in there, I guess I'd lost some confidence. I wanted to re-assess my own evaluation of myself. More than anything, I wanted to prove to myself that I could play football.

GREEN BAY

I met Vince Lombardi when I checked into the Packers' training camp at St. Norbert College in De Pere, Wisconsin, not far from Green Bay. He was standing outside the dormitory greeting all the rookies as they came in, looking happy and showing all his teeth. When I walked up, he said, "Boy, you're a big one," like, Wait 'til I get hold of you.

I was ready—as much as anybody could be—for a Lombardi camp. I had worked out that summer in Louisville with Lenny Lyles, who played for the Colts, Ernie Green, who was with the Browns, and a couple of others.

43

I'D RATHER BE WRIGHT

I had been drafted as a defensive end so they tried to show me what would be expected of me. Lyles gave me some advice: Don't mess with the veterans, just say "Yes, sir" or "No, sir." They'll be trying to screw you because you'll be trying to take their jobs away from them.

It turned out that it wasn't like that at all in Green Bay. It was just the opposite. The veterans couldn't do enough for you. That's one reason why the Packers were so distinctive.

When I got up there, Forrest Gregg was the starting right tackle, an All-Pro, and Forrest took me under his wing and showed me everything he could. Once he told me, "There's only one thing that counts and that's winning. If you can take my job away from me, if you're better than I am, then you deserve to be out there playing instead of me." Amazing, but that's the way the Packer team was. As long as you were willing to learn and to work, every one of them would help you.

They tried me first as a defensive end, and that was a disaster. I lasted one day. I didn't even know how to get in the proper stance. At Alabama, I had played defensive end just like a linebacker plays his position, in a two-point stance, just standing up.

So when I lined up, they didn't know what to make of me. We were doing the nutcracker drill, which is strictly one-on-one. The defensive lineman is supposed to beat the offensive lineman, then tackle the ball carrier. Well, they looked at my stance like they couldn't believe it, like, This is a fifth-round draft choice? What are you doing?

Right then I knew where I was, in a world of trouble. I was getting knocked down and all the ball carriers were running right over me.

A couple of guys were doing even worse and they were dropped from the team that first day. They just weren't in shape. They had the misconception you had to put on weight to make it in the pros, so they just blew themselves right up to 250 or 260 and then couldn't handle the workouts. I did better the second day. They tried me at offensive tackle, and that was one thing I could do, block.

The first friend I made was Ken Bowman, then a rookie center. He had a knack for getting into trouble, too. They had a pre-training camp training camp that year, mostly for centers, quarterbacks, and receivers. On the very first day Bowman asked Bob Skoronski, the regular center, who that baldheaded old man was on the sideline. It turned out to be Henry Jordan, the all-pro defensive tackle. That endeared Bowman to all the veterans right away. And they didn't forget it for a long time.

Jordan was something special. He typified the Packer spirit. He was easy going, a great guy. He'd help you any way he could, with business, with broads, with your home life, anything. He played with the Packers for thirteen years and a couple of times toward the end he thought about retiring. No wonder. He had back trouble and he used to get all doubled up with cramps on hot days. They used to straighten him out by hanging him up on a door. Really. They'd do it in the locker room or in his room at the dormitory. I can still remember ol' Henry just hanging up there.

Another old-timer, Hawg Hanner, was something else, too, a lot like Jordan, always willing to help. He lived in West Memphis, Arkansas, drove a pickup truck up to Green Bay, and went out to practice and everywhere else with a whole pack of Beechnut chewing tobacco in his jaw.

Once he went to see Jerry Kramer while Kramer was in the hospital and when the nun there saw the side of Hanner's face she went berserk. Wanted to get him a wheelchair and everything. Thought he had some serious illness. They'd never seen a jaw that big.

Hawg was a huge man, about 275, and like Jordan he was a defensive tackle. You could never get under him to block him, he was like a big frog, so if you were leading a play you knew it would have to go over both you and Hawg.

His last year was my rookie one and the heat at that training camp was unbearable. It was like 98 degrees, I never saw it like that in Wisconsin again, and Hawg was dying. He has fair skin and a ruddy complexion and his face would turn beet red. I thought the grass drills were going to kill him.

46

I'D RATHER BE WRIGHT

They were Vince's special torture. Whenever you saw him smile, you knew it was the beginning of the grass drills. We did them after the regular calisthenics and before the regular practice. You'd run in place, picking your knees up as high as you could, then Vince would yell "front" and you'd hit the ground prone and then he'd yell "up" and you'd do a quick push up. There's no rhythm to the ups and downs and this is what really gets you. The record was 164 of them, one of the coaches kept count. Somehow, everybody survived.

Vince would walk among the players during the drill, he really enjoyed that. He'd look at people and yell, "Pick 'em up higher . . . Run faster . . . You're not getting up fast enough . . . Faster."

You'd follow his eyes and when his back was to you, if you were a veteran, you could cheat, because none of the other coaches would scream at the veterans, only at the rookies. If Vince would say "down," but he wasn't looking at you, you'd just take a little dip and never really go down. But as a rookie, you'd have to do them all.

During the rare times he gave us a rest, he'd still be walking through this mass of humanity stretched out on the ground and he'd be constantly talking, telling all of us that you never got anything for nothing, you gotta work for everything you get and, okay, it's the fourth quarter, now you really gotta go, you're tired, your guts are hanging out, let's go.

47

I remember Marv Fleming got some of his ribs cracked in a game one Sunday and on Tuesday he was out running pass patterns anyway. But that wasn't good enough for Vince. He was screaming at Fleming to "Move, forget about that cracked rib, you don't even need it. That rib can't hurt you. You can't hurt the human body." That was Vincent, "You can't hurt the human body. It's the greatest machine ever made."

So you never quit, even in practice. Once I got hit in the head with a forearm and went through the whole practice with a concussion. I was in a fog and I didn't start to come out of it until I got in the shower and I was talking to Forrest. I asked him, "Do we have to go back out today?" I kept thinking it was the first day of training camp and that we had two-a-day practices. Actually, it was the third or fourth week of the season. Forrest says, "You sure you're all right?" I said, "I don't know," so he took me in to see the trainer.

The next day the other guys covered for me at practice, they knew something was the matter. They'd say "Hey, you want me to take your turn, Steve?" And Forrest would say, "Just take it easy." So I stayed on the sideline and tried to get my head cleared. I think I went in for a couple of plays when Vince came over close to watch because, remember, you can't hurt the human body. But, again, if somebody was injured, or hung over from the night before, you'd cover for him. It was nothing more than Vince preached, to love your fellow man.

As a rookie, I was totally in awe of the Packer veterans. I lived with one of them, Doug Hart, in a house outside of town. Doug liked to play cards and since he was single the poker club was at our house. Jimmy Taylor would come over, as well as Jerry Kramer, Urban Henry, Bob Skoronski, and Paul Hornung.

There was $800 in the pot for the first hand, just for openers. I didn't gamble anyway, but that clinched it. No way I was gonna get into that, I'd have blown half a year's salary in the first three hands.

I was happy just to watch. I was standing around dazed one night, seeing nothing but twenties and fifties and hundreds in a big pile. You gotta realize this is my rookie year, and I'm a kid from Alabama. A hundred dollar bill, are you kidding me? There's this great big stack of them there and all I can think of is grabbing that money and running, man.

Not only am I no gambler, I'm a born loser. Max McGee pointed that out to me. One time we were on a bus going somewhere and Max says, "All right, I've got a card. It's black, and it's between a seven and a nine. What is it?" I said the eight of clubs. He says, "Wright, you should never gamble. When you can't hit the fifty-fifty shots forget it." Max could hit 'em.

I'd say he could hit eight out of ten fifty-fifty shots but I'm the kind of guy who walks up to a double door and picks the locked one.

The first time I was out with the veterans was in Milwaukee, and I thought I was really big time. I went downtown and bought a Stetson hat and that night I found a girl in town, picked her up, and went over to a place called the Whiskey Au Go-Go.

It had a back room and all the Packers were there: Hornung, Jerry Kramer, Jim Taylor, Ron Kramer, Dan Curry, Max McGee, Fuzzy Thurston, the whole crowd. I walked back there with my date, and that was the last time I saw either the hat or her.

Curry grabbed the hat, maybe because he was the slowest. The other guys grabbed the chick. I think five of them handled her in two minutes. About that time Hornung ordered a round for everybody and threw out a hundred on the table. A few minutes later somebody else threw down another hundred. I'm looking at these hundreds and thinking, Son of a bitch, I'm worrying about a $15 hat.

That's how the Packers were, free-wheelers, big spenders. They were football at the time, kind of giants who trod the earth, you could feel it everywhere. And Hornung was the Packers. Anywhere Paul went the broads were there. He didn't have to worry about getting laid if he wanted to. He had his choice. He didn't have to worry about buying a drink because there were always drinks, people buying drinks on top of drinks.

It was that way in Green Bay, Milwaukee, Chicago, you name it, wherever we went. When we were in Florida for the Super Bowl I was talking to a chick and Hornung walked up to her and said, "Play your cards right and you'll get laid by Paul Hornung tonight." That's the way it was.

In Green Bay, you managed to have fun the best way you could. You had to do something because there was so much work, and the mental pressure during the season was just unbearable, seven days a week. You could make every play perfect in a game except one and that one would be all you'd think about from the time the game ended Sunday until Tuesday when Vince started screaming at you. For the rest of Sunday and all day Monday and Tuesday until you got to the films and got chewed out you'd keep wanting to get it over with.

So you'd do something, anything, to keep your sanity: play cards, drink, pick up a girl. There was always a friendly bartender somewhere. If there were 500 stores in Green Bay 400 of them were bars. And there were always plenty of girls available. Not the best looking honeys sometimes, but plenty of them. Let's face it, it's so cold up there you gotta do something to keep warm.

I had a good setup one year. Hart got married so I moved into a small apartment complex. The local fun girl was right next door. All you had to do was knock on the wall. The next year she moved out and Bob Long, a straight-arrow type, moved in. For months he was besieged by drunks banging on his door at four in the morning wondering where the girl was.

If you wanted to go out, there were a few decent places, but there just wasn't that much privacy. In Green Bay, everybody knew everybody else's business, and this was a hell of a problem. I could take a girl home with me and not say anything to anybody, because that's the way I am. My business is my business. But three people still might walk up to me on the street, people I just knew casually, and they'd tell me who I was with the night before. No wonder Vince always knew where we were and what we were doing.

I guess the word got back about Hornung a few times, too, but with Vince, Hornung was different. They had a special relationship and Vince would bend for Paul. He was the Prodigal Son. I think it went back to their first year together. There was Hornung, the Heisman Trophy winner out of Notre Dame, but he hadn't done anything with the Packers. So Vince comes along and puts Paul where he thinks he should be, at halfback instead of quarterback. It was like the first crisis they went through together, and it worked. Paul was playing football again, which is what he wanted to do, and Vince had himself a hell of a running back. If it hadn't worked, we might not have heard much about either of them.

52

To me, football ended when Vince died. I haven't found anybody who comes close to him, and I don't think I will. He set his goals and he worked toward them with more dedication than anyone I ever met. The way he went about it made a lot of people mad, but he did what he thought was right.

I think Vince could have been one of the nicest guys in the world. He probably was at one time. I can imagine him as just an easy-going, average John Q. Public. But he wanted more. He loved football, and he wanted to be the best.

And his philosophy was: To be the best you've got to give up a whole heck of a lot. You can't spread yourself too thin, you've got to concentrate on one thing. You never get something for nothing, you've got to decide what you want to give up.

You knew he was serious and you knew just what to expect from him. He wasn't the kind of guy who was up one day and down the next and maybe a little bit in between the next day. You knew what he was gonna be like all the time.

He always used to say there were only three important things: your family, your religion, and the Green Bay Packers. But those three things were synonymous to Vince. Sure, he was a dedicated Catholic, he went to Mass every morning. But, really, his religion was the Green Bay Packers. His family was the Green Bay Packers. Football was the Green Bay Packers.

I have to give a lot of credit to Marie, his wife, for

putting up with all this stuff because, let's face it, he had to be a tyrant coming home after watching some of those game films. As far as I'm concerned, he gave up the role of Vince Lombardi, nice guy, family man, for Vince Lombardi, dominant figure of football.

I guess the oldest joke about Vince was the one where he goes home and gets in bed with Marie and she says, "God, your feet are cold," and he says, "When we're at home you can call me Vince." But some people really looked at Vince that way, as a god. And I think, at the height of his career, he might have looked at himself a little bit that way. He believed in everything he did and he felt that if you believed in what he was doing, too, both of you would benefit by it.

He saw himself as the personification of the Green Bay Packers, which is why he reacted so violently if anybody said anything derogatory about the team. Lombardi and the Packers were synonymous. They still are today.

And yet when he died, the Packers wouldn't pay for an airplane to take all the players to New York for the funeral and, let's face it, he made the organization what it is. I think they made $700,000 the year before he left so you know they could afford to spend a little money for something like that.

In my own mind, I like to compare Vince to Alexander the Great who was asked, Do you want a long life of obscurity or a short life of fame? I guess that was the most human aspect of Lombardi, that he wanted fame, and like a lot of people he enjoyed it.

He made it plain in his little talks that he wasn't going to allow you to embarrass him by your play. "I'm the coach of this team and you're not gonna embarrass me. I'll pull you out at halftime. I won't let you on the field to start with."

So I respected him, but I didn't fear him. I could see what he was doing, manipulating us toward an end. But I felt it was a good end. I believe, as he did, you never get something for nothing. I'll work as hard as anybody. But there has to be a purpose in anything I do. With Vince, there always was.

If he told you to do something, the team would benefit by it. He wouldn't say go out there and run and just keep running 'til you drop. He might tell you to run because you're not in shape and you knew right then, Hey, if he says I'm not in shape, I'm not in shape and he's got 10 guys waiting to take my place.

He created pride through his training camps. Anyone who has worked hard for something is less apt to give in. That's why he beat the shit out of us physically and mentally in camp. When we walked out on the field for a game, we knew we were the best, we knew we were prepared and that we were going to win. There was no doubt in anybody's mind. He would say, "Are you going to waste all that sweat and time on the field last summer?" Uh-uh.

For example, no one doubted that we were going

to come from behind and win that NFL title game with Dallas, the one up in Green Bay in 1967 when the temperature was minus 13. That was the way you felt when you were a Packer. If you get down near the goal line you're gonna get across. Vince always stressed that.

Incidentally, this isn't knocking Jerry Kramer, but the man who made the touchdown play go, when Bart Starr sneaked over in the final seconds of that game was Ken Bowman. Kramer hitting Jethro Pugh has become almost an historic block, but in the films you can see Kramer hit and slide off. If Bowman hadn't cleaned up, Pugh would have given Bart a big kiss.

In addition to the work, the training camps served another purpose: to bring everybody together. You can all want to do well as individuals, but if you're not united you can't succeed. Vince had the toughest camps but when you got through them, when it finally got down to the forty men, he knew there'd be a feeling of comradeship among them. Love for each other, he called it. Whatever it was, you were willing to do something, to go out of your way for your teammate for no other reason than the fact that he was your teammate. I've never found that any place else.

Vince would demand emotion and would always bring up the notion that you're playing for each other, you're playing for the Packers, and you know good and well the other team has no right being on the field with you, so go out there and run 'em off.

The thing that bugged Vince about me more than anything was that I never showed my feelings. I never let anyone know what I was thinking. And I guess sometimes it looked like I wasn't thinking about anything. He said repeatedly, "I want people who wear their emotions on their sleeve." This is not me.

I think he realized that after a while and understood that you have to make allowances for some people. He was a strict disciplinarian, yet he was able to bend enough because he had an end: He wanted to win football games. It didn't make any difference to him what you looked like, where you came from or what you did in the off-season, just as long as when you walked on that field with a Packer uniform on, you were the best.

To that end, he could embarrass you so much that your first reaction would be, I'm gonna show that son of a bitch, which is just what he wanted you to do. One of the first games I got into as a rookie was against Dallas. I was up against George Andrie and I had this doubt in my mind, Can I do it? Maybe I can't do it.

The first play was right over me and I fired out and hit George and I bounced right back on my ass. Well, Vince ran that piece of film back and forth five times. It cracked up the meeting. In my stance, hit him, on the ground, hit him, in my stance, hit him, on the ground.

Vince knew it was because of my indecision. How many times had I done it before then? That's why he went berserk. "You wouldn't be here if you couldn't block. Now what kind of a block is that? What do you have, a rubber band on you?"

Yet, every once in a while, two or three times a year, he'd come up, put his arm around me, and tell me in essence that he thought I was a good football player, that he knew everybody was a little different. He'd take me on a little ego trip, that's what it amounted to. I guess that's one reason I love him.

During the 1965 season I was starting and playing well and then I got injured. I had my foot stepped on in a game against Los Angeles in Milwaukee. It hurt but I didn't think much of it, just kept on playing. You know, you can't hurt the human body. The next day it hurt more and more and by Tuesday I could barely walk.

But I kept on going—if you're hurt you keep it to yourself and work it out the best way you can—and two weeks later we played the Rams again, at Los Angeles. Deacon Jones just picked me up and threw me away and tackled Zeke Bratkowski in the end zone for a safety and they pulled me out of there and reshuffled the line. That was it for me for the rest of the season.

It turned out there was a calcium deposit in my foot which had crushed some cartilage, so I had to have an operation after the season. When I took the insurance form into Vince so the Packers could pay for it, he said, "Why didn't you say something about this?"

You can imagine what his reaction would have been had I actually said anything at the time. But now it was a quiet moment and Vince was sympathetic. I said, "I didn't think it was that bad but I knew I wasn't playing as well as I should have been." And he said, "I noticed that. You went downhill all of a sudden. I couldn't figure it out."

In other words, to Vince, there had to be a reason if somebody was playing badly because there just weren't any bad players on the Packers in those days. In his speeches about pride he always said to take pride in the guy next to you. Don't let anybody tell you that guy's no good, because he is or he wouldn't be here.

With the Packers, you thought first of the team, and you actually hated to let the other guys down. I can remember really being embarrassed by a freak injury. We were playing in Milwaukee, it was a pass block play, I'm dropping back, and somebody comes in about a second or two late and hits me on the knee. It was like somebody took a hammer and went bam. I went right down and I couldn't move. It felt like my knee wasn't there. I couldn't even crawl off the field. I took two hobbles on my good leg and fell over. They had to call time out and get the trainer out to me.

So there you are sitting in the middle of the field with 50,000 people looking down wondering what that big clown is doing and all you want to do is get back in the huddle. But you can't move. Can't hurt the human body, eh? Fantastic salesman, Vince.

If he had been born 500 years ago, he'd have conquered the world. He'd have had an army feeling the same way. Not an army of people saying, I wish to hell I was out of here, but one that was saying, We're the best in the world, no one can defeat us. This was the way we were on the Packers. I'm afraid I'm getting too serious, but I get hung up on this stuff 'cause I dig Vince.

I may have loved Lombardi, but I sure had a knack for getting him pissed off. And I mean pissed. He'd scream at me in the team meetings, I was one of his favorites. Invariably he had the evidence against me, right there on film. We used to joke about it afterward, on the way to the field for practice. Forrest Gregg would look at me and say, "Well, you got the Oscar again today, didn't you."

One time they filmed a scrimmage and Willie Davis just ate me alive. I didn't know which end was up. Vince would keep running the film over and over and getting madder and madder and I'm just sitting there smiling, unconsciously, really, and he'd yell, "Goddamn it, Wright, wipe that silly smirk off your face." Like I couldn't do anything right.

Just once I got lucky. We had played Baltimore, it was 1965, and it was Hornung's last big game. He scored five touchdowns. And he did it all with no help from me, that's for sure. I was awful. My knees were killing me that day, tendonitis or something. I mean I was in pain, I was dying every time I was in there. But it was foggy, so foggy you couldn't see from one end of the field to the other. It was so foggy the films didn't turn out. Vince couldn't see a thing.

Usually, though, I would be right up there on the screen in black and white, and Vince would go berserk. Three times that year, for some reason I pulled the wrong way on the famous Green Bay sweep. Knocked down two guards, a center, and a tackle. Boy, were they surprised to see me coming right at them. Kenny Bowman nicknamed me Bullwinkle for that, for Bullwinkle Moose of the TV show, "Rocky and His Friends." If you've heard the line by Bullwinkle you'll know why. "Go, go, go, but watch where you're going."

The first time it happened Vince just accepted it, but the second time he went crazy, and the third time he was just livid, unbelievable. He stopped the projector, stood up, turned the lights on, and started chewing me out.

"What's the matter with you, Wright, can't you hear? The play's thirty-eight, not thirty-nine. Eight and nine, they don't even sound alike.

"Bart, say eight." So Bart says "Eight." Then Vince says, "Now say nine." Bart says "Nine."

"Now they don't sound alike, do they, Wright?"

"No, Coach."

"Well, why'd you do it?"

"I don't know why, Coach."

He had the projector stopped and was screaming at me for three or four minutes, which is a hell of a long time.

But the worst temper tantrum he ever had was out on the field at practice, and naturally it happened because of me. It turned out that he was bothered by it more than I was. I didn't realize the effect it had until he wrote about it in an article for *Look* magazine (September 5, 1967).

This is what he wrote:

> We were all out on that field across Oneida Street from Lambeau Field, and suddenly I was rushing at one of my players and flailing away at him with my fists. I am 54 years old now, and he is eight inches taller than I am and outweighs me by 50 pounds. If he had brought both of his hands down on me, he probably could have driven me into the ground, but he just stood there, warding off my blows because he understands me. Fortunately, all of the Packers understand me.
>
> What was I doing? Did I hate him, or

even dislike him? No, not for a moment. I'm fond of him. He's one of the most likable men on our squad. That's his problem. He has all the size and ability he needs to be a great one, but he loves everybody. In a game, they beat on him. Everybody whacks him, and he laughs. When you criticize him, he laughs, so what was I doing? I guess I was trying to reach him in the only way left. I guess I was trying to get him to hate me enough to take it out on the opposition, because to play the game, you must have fire in you, and there is nothing that strokes that fire like hate.

I'm sorry, but that is the truth.

To put it in perspective, Vince wasn't in a good mood to start with. Two or three days earlier we had had a bad practice and I had busted a play and, to Vince, busting a play in practice was the same as busting a play in a game. You just don't do it. I'm looking at him out of the corner of my eye and I can see he's looking right at me and he's saying, "Don't you smile, Wright, don't let me see you smile, I'll run you off this field right now if I see you smile."

So I suppose I was fresh in his mind a couple of days later when we had another bad practice. We were standing in the huddle when he came charging up and just started ranting and raving, and all of a sudden he turned and looked right at me. It was one of those things. I just happened to be in the wrong place at the wrong time and I was looking at him and our eyes met and I had a kind of blank expression on my face. I think that made him even madder.

He was saying something and he just broke off the sentence and directed all his wrath at me: "You, you, who do you think you are? You could be the greatest tackle in the world but you don't care, do you?"

And there he was beating on my chest. And I'm looking down at him like, What're you doing? Go away. I actually laughed and tried to push him away. I got to laughing and I couldn't stop and this made him even madder.

Three times he started pounding on me and three times I pushed him back. He'd hit me and I'd push him away, he'd hit me and I'd push him away.

None of the other guys said anything. Just silence. But you could tell from their faces what they were thinking. It was like, Well, you did it again, didn't you, Wright? I don't have to go looking for trouble. It's easy to find.

Like this other time before a game. About forty minutes before the kickoff most of us would go out to warm up, then come back in, do whatever we had to do, and get our pads on. That day it was just one of those times when I had to go to the bathroom.

So I was sitting in there reading the newspaper and doing my thing, making it an enjoyable experience, and when I was done I walked out into the locker room with my pants still down around my knees. As soon as I got there I knew something was wrong. All of the players were at one end of the room and Vince was right in the middle of them.

He turned around and saw me and right then I knew I should never have come out. I guess I had flushed the toilet right at the dramatic high point of his spiel and he just started yelling at me. "What are we running here, a goddamn nursery? Can't you do anything right, Wright?"

I guess the answer to that is no. I used to sit up in the front row during the team meetings. Now there's no way you can get in trouble up there, right? You can't go to sleep in front of him. How can you go wrong? I found a way.

There I was up front, right on the aisle—he had already chewed me out about five times—and he started to walk backwards while he was explaining something and he tripped over one of my big feet.

Now he was really frustrated. "Wright," he bellowed, "I just can't get away from you."

I could even get the most mild-mannered people mad at me. Like Phil Bengtson, the defensive coach who eventually succeeded Lombardi. Good head as far as defenses go, a good tactician, but as far as inspiring someone, no. That was part of the Packers' problems after Vince retired. The change was too abrupt. Phil was far too easy-going.

I can't remember him losing his temper at anybody,

except me. That's why it surprised me. I was in the wedge on the kickoff team and one day we were out on the field practicing the formation, and Phil was in charge. I was talking to Lionel Aldridge and I guess Phil thought I wasn't paying any attention to him.

Wouldn't you know it, this was one time I was really serious. I was asking Lionel how far apart we should be standing, and I got crucified for it. Bengston literally chased me off the field. Boy, did he get mad.

Then there was Bart Starr. Bart is the nicest guy in the world. I mean, you can't believe someone is like this. This guy blows his nose, too, right? He's truly charitable. He's helped promote a program called Rawhide to help abandoned children by providing them a home.

The guys on the team, and people in general, would come to him for advice, money, anything. He's the fatherly type. I think the worst chewing out he ever got from Vince was, "What's the matter, couldn't you read that defense, Bart?" And Bart would say, "No, Coach," and that was it.

Well, Bart got a little upset at me once during a game against Pittsburgh. I was up against Lloyd Voss and Lloyd just came barreling in, picked me up, and almost took me back to say hello to Bart. He got the pass away, no problem, but we were kind of close to him and I guess it annoyed him.

He came back to the huddle and said, "Steve

Wright, you should be ashamed of yourself, letting a player like Lloyd Voss do that to you. If he does that again, I'm going to kick you in the butt." That was about the strongest language Bart ever used.

Zeke Bratkowski, the backup quarterback, was the same type of person. Well, almost, I heard Zeke say damn one time.

Maybe because he wanted to reform me, Vince had me room in camp and on the road with Tom Brown, a hell of a nice guy, solid citizen type. Didn't help a bit, did it?

Tom was the kind of guy you'd see at the start of camp and you'd say, "Good to see you, Tom, how are you?" He'd say, "Fine," and that was it—for the season. Tom just never said anything to anybody. It was sort of a standing joke, people would ask, "How's Brown this year?" and I'd say, "Oh, he's really loosened up. He said, 'Fine. How are you?'"

On the road, early in the season, we'd race to get to the room first because if I got there I'd turn on a Saturday afternoon movie. If he got there first he'd turn on a baseball game. And I hate baseball with a passion. I think it's the most boring thing you can watch. But he had played for the Washington Senators —talk about boring—for a while and he could just sit there for hours watching a stupid, goddamn baseball game. And if there was more than one game, forget it. I'd just take off and roam the streets or something.

But one time we actually had a conversation. I had met this girl from Green Bay and we had had some great times together so I started talking with Tom about marriage. He recommended it highly, telling me how great it is, that you have to settle down sometime, have a nice life, and the whole bit.

So I got married. I've been pissed off at him ever since. I should have listened to Kenny Bowman. He was my best man and he drove me to the church. About a block and a half before we got there he stopped the car and said, "This is your last chance." I blew it.

Well, I hadn't been married long when I was offered an off-season job and I figured, Hell, I'll go the whole route, marriage, work, a nice little house. So I got into glue. Yeah, glue. The Everseal Industrial Glue Co. was looking for a salesman up in the Wisconsin area, so for some reason they tried to get Ray Nitschke, the Packers' middle linebacker. Ray didn't want the job so I took it.

Anyway, if you can imagine the least likely salesman in the world it would be Ray Nitschke. He's the kind of guy who would walk in your office, throw down a hunk of glue in front of you, and say, "You want some glue? Here. Buy it."

Another great talker was Jimmy Taylor, our fullback. He could double talk, and he used to get Vince furious. You wouldn't know it by looking at him, hard as a rock, a fantastic runner, give him a wall and

68

he'd go through it, but Jimmy was a bit of a practical joker. He loved to smoke cigars in the meetings because it blew Vince's mind. Vince couldn't stand it. Vince would scream, "Taylor, put that goddamn cigar out," he didn't have to turn the lights on or anything, he knew who it was.

Then Vince would be watching the film and all of a sudden, "Taylor, look at that. Do you know what you're doing? Why did you do that? Why? Why?"

"Uh, well, Coach, I was going around and I cut to the right and he was standing there right in front of me and I didn't know which way to go because I saw his fromish and then his kribish and when the tackle froused, you know, it happened so quick."

And everybody's there sitting in the dark almost cracking up, you can hear them trying not to laugh, and Vince is saying, "What? Does anybody understand what he's saying?" I don't know if Vince ever caught on. I think he just stopped asking Jimmy questions.

When it comes to the big games, I remember the strangest things. Take the title game of 1967, the one we played against Dallas at thirteen below zero up in Green Bay.

They built dugouts for us on the sidelines and installed these big hot air blowers to keep us warm. Well, along with the hot air we were getting these goddamn diesel fumes and it was smelling like the back end of a bus. Then, right in the middle of the game, something happened to one of the blowers. It just ran out of gas or something, and white clouds of smoke went all through the dugout. We all jumped up and ran out of there. We didn't know whether the thing was on fire or what.

Everyone was milling around trying to figure out if it was safe to go back in there when Bob Skoronski gets hurt and they start screaming for me to go in. But I don't have my helmet. I can't find it. It's lost. And they're screaming, Wright, hey Wright, because it's right in the middle of the game, and my helmet's somewhere in the dugout in all that smoke. I'm tearing around in there looking, they're yelling, and I can't find the damn thing so finally I turn around and Lionel Aldridge gives me his helmet.

It's about a half-size too big, and it's wobbling all over my head while I'm running out on the field, and when I buckle the chin strap it hangs way down. And, why I don't know, they call the next three plays right over me. First of all I'm freezing cold, my system is like molasses, I can't move. And I'm looking at that ground and it's like concrete. Hitting it would be like diving into an empty swimming pool, only worse.

So when we come up to the line of scrimmage I'm opposite the Cowboys' George Andrie, and as I bend over to take my stance that's the last I see of him. Aldridge's helmet falls right down on my nose and I can't see anything except the ground. Oh, I don't wanna hit that ground. When I do, the skin comes off both elbows, the helmet rolls over my head and bounces down the field, I cut down Andrie, and we make three or four yards.

It took about five plays—every time a play begins the helmet is covering my face—to get off the field, find my own helmet, and get myself together, and Lombardi is just standing there looking at me like, You're a football player?

Besides all that, I was literally shaking while I was in there, not from the cold, but from nerves. I have a habit, I guess it's tension more than anything else, but when I get down in my stance the first few times my legs shake. This can be disastrous for an offensive tackle, because you can't move once you're down.

In the first Super Bowl against Kansas City, in Los Angeles, I was really worried because you just don't get penalties in the Super Bowl, especially for a nervous twitch in your leg. I didn't want to cost everybody on the team a $15,000 payday. That trip was all business, especially because we were supposedly defending the prestige of the National Football League against the upstart American. When we got out to the Coast, Vince said, "Curfew's at 11 o'clock. If you find somebody you want to go out with after 11 o'clock it's going to cost you the game check if I catch you." Then he added, "If you do find somebody worth that much, take me along because I want to meet her." That was the last bit of levity until we walked off the field with a 35-10 victory and one of the Chiefs said to Elijah Pitts, "We're better than you guys." And Elijah said dryly. "Then how come we got more points on the board?"

The second Super Bowl was like the end of an era. We had accomplished what no other team had, three straight NFL championships, and that would be the second Super Bowl victory, and the word was going around the team that Vince was going to retire from coaching and become general manager.

He had done everything. What more could he do? Also, I think he knew the team had had it, that it couldn't be pushed any more. A lot of the older players had had it, too, with the pressure, with all of the football, with the screaming and the ranting and raving. They wanted to start enjoying themselves. They were beginning to accumulate business interests and were thinking about things besides football.

I think Vince felt that he had accomplished everything he set out to do, that he couldn't do anything now but ruin everything he'd done if he pushed it any farther. So he pretty much told us in the locker room before the second Super Bowl that it was the last game for him, that he was going to step down. It was all the incentive we needed. We beat Oakland easily, 33-14.

Because we won the championship every year, we'd automatically have to play another "big" game the following summer, against the College All-Stars, in Chicago. It was a pain in the ass. These kids would play their guts out and you'd just toy with 'em because you could really mess 'em up if you wanted to. You'd play just well enough to win.

Late in the afternoon, before the '66 game, a friend of mine called me at the hotel and said to come on over to Trader Vic's and have a drink. I had about three Navy Grogs and when I got on the field I was feeling no pain. I wasn't drunk, I was just feeling good.

Ken Bowman and I and about three other guys were standing around during the pre-game practice and Ken looks at me and says, "Somebody's been drinking. Can you smell it?"

I breathed right in his face and said, "Noooo." He just looked at me and shook his head.

By no means was I the biggest drinker on the team. Uh-uh, not with Hornung around. Fuzzy Thurston could hold his own, too. When Fuzzy, Max McGee, and Hornung got together it was really like the Three Stooges. Nothing, I mean nothing, would shake these guys up. You name it, they'd do it.

Hornung, he'd like to take off at least his shirt—I heard he once got down to his shorts—and get up on top of a bar and dance with a martini on top of his head. What a show. Must be the shape of his head.

Max and Paul were always on the telephone, in and out of the dorm at camp at all hours. Once we went down to Dallas for a Sunday night game and when we got back to Green Bay the next day the headline in the sports section was, "Warrant Issued For McGee's Arrest." Big black print, you couldn't miss it.

It turns out the night before we left for Dallas, Max sneaked out of the dormitory and drove to Manitowoc where he has a restaurant, The Left End, and coming back he got stopped by the police for speeding and was ordered to appear in court Monday morning. Monday morning we were still in Dallas.

So it cost him $1000 for sneaking out of the dorm, plus court costs, but this was typical of him, you know, what's a thousand? You win some, you lose some. This was the way all three of them were. You want to fine me $500? Okay, fine me.

After Lombardi quit coaching, there wasn't any reason to stay around Green Bay. I had gotten a divorce. And I wasn't making that much money. I thought it was time for a change of scenery.

I had asked for a raise but they wouldn't give it to me. In fact, Pat Peppler, the guy who handled signings, actually laughed at me. I was making $14,500 a season, only $2,500 more than when I started four years before. I asked for $18,000 and it was like I was asking for $50,000. He asked me if I was serious.

You bet I was. A couple of years before, they had signed up this kid, Dave Dunaway, a receiver from Duke, to a no-cut contract. Somebody said he was making about $26,000. He came in with a fairly good reputation but I don't think he caught a ball at training camp. They sent him home about three quarters of the way through the season. So if they can pay that much for a guy who didn't do anything, I must be worth a little something. I'd been there four years beating my brains out. Naturally, I wanted more money.

A lot of the older guys wanted more, especially when they paid Donny Anderson and Jim Grabowski a total of $1 million. The veterans had been making the money for the organization to pay for these two kids, and you couldn't blame them for feeling the way they did. Anderson's contract for something like $700,000 was unprecedented.

Namath earned every bit of his money. He won his teammates' respect. As for Donny Anderson, he's got to be the highest paid punter in history. Can you see paying $700,000 to kick a ball? I don't care how far he kicks it.

So I just wanted to get out of there. I told my line coach, Ray Wietecha, that I wanted to be traded. Was it a mistake? You bet it was, baby. I had no idea what it was like on other teams. I really asked for it.

About a month passed and I got a call in Milwaukee, where I was busy selling glue. It was that coach, what's his name? I can't think of his name. That must tell you something. Oh, yeah, Phil Bengtson. Bengtson told me I'd been traded. I was off to New York and all kinds of fun and games.

NEW YORK

I got into trouble in New York because I tried to reform the entire Giant organization. I couldn't believe that a football team could be as fucked up as the New York Giants. There was no team unity. Nobody trusted anybody else. I mean, it really shook me, especially since I came from Green Bay.

I can't think of anybody on the Packers I didn't like. There wasn't anybody you wouldn't have over to your house for a beer. If somebody got in trouble, everybody else would help. If somebody called up and said he really needed some help, it was, What do you want me to do? You could call thirty people and say, Look, I'm in a spot, could you take care of this for me? And if they couldn't do it, they knew somebody who could, and it would get done.

In New York, forget it. On the Giants, it was, I've got this to do and I've got that to do and look, how about calling somebody else. Nobody wanted to help anybody. Once I called somebody to ask if I could borrow his car to pick up a girl at Kennedy Airport and he said, I gotta go pick up my cleaning. Really. This was the accepted thing at New York.

There was a general distrust by everybody of everyone else on the team. Nobody—players, coaches, management—trusted anybody. I'd never seen anything like it. It wasn't at all like the "family" Lombardi taught the Packers to be.

It wasn't any mystery to me why the Giants were losing. I knew what it took to have a winning team. I learned all about that at Green Bay. So I tried the best way I could to help get the Giants together. You have to do, at least I have to do, what you think is right. So I tried, and I got suspended.

For two weeks, the length of my suspension, I got more press in New York than the President. I didn't accept the treatment I got, I fought it, because there was really no legitimate reason for my suspension.

I could write a book about the Giants. It would be three thousand pages long and all of them would be blank except for four words on the first page, "Don't

Rock the Boat." But I rocked it. If I had been the good little New York Football Giant, I'd probably still be there now.

I'm glad I'm not though, and it comes right down to this: I can't stand phony people, and the Giants had too many of them for me. They were always trying to be somebody to one person and somebody else to another, and this is what got me in trouble because I'm me anywhere I go, I'm exactly the same. I know bums and I know millionaires and I'm the same with both. I'm as at home in Levis as I am in a tux, I don't try to come on two different ways.

The club was full of cliques, the most significant being the Tucker Frederickson clique. That's all I heard about before and after I got there, how Tucker could do this and Tucker could do that, and I haven't seen him do anything yet. For most people, Tucker was easy to like. He was always having parties and it was someplace to go and there were always broads over there. Except I'm the kind of guy who asks, What are you doing for the team?

Then there was the omnipotent Wellington Mara. As Red Smith said, "Wellington was born naked into the world and had to inherit everything he has," namely the New York Giants' football team and he's playing it to the hilt. Who does he think he is? He's never been on a football field except to put on his New York Giant sweatshirt and run around and do ten sit-ups and go to banquets and say, Yes, I'm

Wellington Mara from the New York Football Giants, my father was a bookie, that's how I got to be the president of the team.

When he fired Allie Sherman as coach, Wellington had a little meeting with the team and he came up with this quote, "The reason we're not winning football games is because we have forty bad football players playing bad football." Can you imagine that, forty bad football players? Who is this guy to be telling us we're bad football players?

Wellington had the players so uptight they were afraid to relax for fear they might say the wrong thing. One of the first things I was told when I got to the Giants was that if you say fuck or shit and Wellington hears you you're in trouble. We wanted forty professional football players to act like a Girl Scout troop.

With an atmosphere like that it's no wonder I got into trouble right away. We were at training camp in Fairfield, Connecticut, when it happened. Every Wednesday night there would be a team cookout. Instead of having a meeting, we would sit around and drink beer and grill steaks, a cozy team get-together.

This one night I was sitting there and this girl I'd met the day before walks by and I invited her to come over and have a beer with us. I didn't think anything about it. Well, you just wouldn't believe the shit I got for doing that.

I walked onto the practice field the next day and

three or four players came up to me saying things like, Boy, are you in trouble.

My first reaction was like, What did I do now?

So they told me. "You had that girl sit down at your table last night."

I said, "Get outta here."

They said, "No, seriously, Wellington doesn't like that."

I'm saying, "You gotta be kidding me."

They say, "No, man, you're in trouble. You better go over to Allie and apologize."

"Get outta here," I keep saying. "What do you mean, go apologize? It's impossible. It just can't be."

Then Allie comes over and says, "I want to talk to you."

I say to myself, It can't be.

Then he takes me aside and says, "I want to talk to you about last night."

I said, "You gotta be shitting me." That's exactly what I told him. I said, "You're telling me that I'm in trouble because I invited a girl to come sit down with me. Nothing happened. We had a thoroughly enjoyable conversation. All we did was sit there and talk. There were fifty-eight guys there and I'm in trouble?"

Allie says, "Well, she's an outsider and we have to lock in when we come out here to Fairfield. This is a team function and we don't want outsiders." One of Allie's favorite expressions was, "We're gonna lock in and we're not gonna cop out. We don't want any cop-outs around here." All you'd have to say to anybody who ever played under Allie is two words, cop out, and he'd automatically know who you were talking about.

So I'm saying, "You're serious about this, aren't you? I mean, we're not kids, we're supposed to be adults, and I'm in trouble because I talked to a girl?"

"I think you owe an apology to the team and to Mr. Mara," he said.

"Okay, who do you want me to apologize to first?"

So the next day I got everybody's attention in the locker room and then I made my apology speech. "I was thoroughly ignorant," I told them, "that I made a boo-boo. I want it known right now that I hereby apologize to all of you for bringing an outsider into your midst."

I kept a straight face. I can do that once in a while. But they laughed. And that was a no-no, too, you're not supposed to laugh. So I guess I got the blame for that too.

Later I went over to Mara's room and apologized again, very seriously. I explained to him that I didn't realize we were all locked in at the time and couldn't see anybody from the outside world.

I told him there were no ulterior motives, that I wasn't trying to make the broad, that she was somebody from Milwaukee, where I was living at the time, that she was there taking some classes and didn't know anybody, and that I was trying to do something nice for someone, a stranger in a new place. Because of that I was in a whole world of trouble.

So he says, "That's all right. We realize you probably didn't know what the rules are. We just don't want it to happen again, Steve."

So I tried, I was on my best behavior for the rest of camp, yet somehow I still managed to get in trouble. For one thing, Rosey Brown, who was coaching the tackles, didn't agree with the way I played my position.

I played four years at Green Bay so I was taught how to play football by someone I consider the greatest offensive tackle, Forrest Gregg. Now Rosey was, to say the least, not the quickest or the most agile of tackles. Strong, yeah, he could take on anybody. He believed in brute strength. I believe in quickness and finesse, because there's no way in the world I'm going to take on a guy who weighs 280 and physically handle him. I'll take him out one way or another, but I'm not going to try to take him on pound for pound or try to outmuscle him because I'd lose, I know this.

So Rosey and I had different philosophies and I tried to play it Rosey's way rather than beat my brains against a wall every practice. One day Allie came up to me and said—and this was typical of Allie—"Steve, I'd like to talk to you for a minute." I knew I hadn't been playing good football so I knew what he wanted to talk about.

His line went like this, "I don't want you to get excited. I don't want you to get nervous or anything. But if you don't play better football this next game, I'm going to trade you."

Beautiful. Like no problem, don't worry about it, don't get nervous, but I'll trade you while your name's still good. Well, I'd been around long enough to know I can play football so I'm just thinking to myself what the hell would happen if he told this to a rookie. That kid's got to be shitting grapefruits.

So I went back and told Rosey that Allie wasn't satisfied with the way I'd been playing, and really I wasn't either, and that I was going to go back to playing ball the way I knew how. And Rosey's comment was, "Okay, just remember one thing. If you get beat playing my way I can stick up for you, but if you get beat playing your way I can't say a thing for you."

Like his word was going to save my job if I was getting beat. I said, "If I get beat, I get beat, whether I'm playing my way or your way, it doesn't make any difference. So I'd rather play it my way." He says, "Okay, but I warned you." Oh man. So I started playing my kind of football and there were no problems.

I didn't think there would be any trouble when I got traded to the Giants. Allie called me in Milwaukee and said that they were happy to have me with them and were looking forward to meeting me and did I have any idea when I would be in New York to see him.

About three or four weeks later I flew to New York and we met and talked. I was impressed with Allie. He seemed like a sincere individual who wanted to win, and I accepted that. We got along fine, we talked contract and I got a substantial raise, to $20,000, which was more than I asked for at Green Bay. *The New York Times* couldn't get over the trade, because the Giants got not only me but Tommy Crutcher, a linebacker, for Francis Peay, a tackle who had been a disappointment. The *Times* called it "a great coup" and even wondered if Lombardi wasn't having compassion for the Giants, his old team.

A couple of weeks before camp, I found an apartment in the city and rented some furniture, but like for two weeks I sat in my room because I had no idea where to go. Really, I should have recognized the situation on the Giants then because I met Tucker Frederickson and Bill Swain. I had Swain's telephone number and I called him up once and I think I went over but it was like hey, don't bother me.

Things started getting really disturbing on the first road trip, ironically to Green Bay. The first thing I was asked when I got on the plane, since the guys really didn't know me, was if I was married. I said no and they said okay, you're all right then, because if you're married and Wellington sees you messing with one of the stewardesses he'll trade you tomorrow. And watch your language or you're in trouble. And don't talk about the game if we lose because Wellington will be mad.

And since Wellington and his friends always sat right there in the middle of the players, this automatically created a feeling of tension throughout the back of the plane. In addition to this, a number of select players like Tucker always sat in first class. Now if I sat there it was made clear to me that, No, you can't sit there, it's my seat. Well, who says it's your seat? I'm going to play out there tomorrow just as much as you are and I'm 6-6 and you're only 5-10 and I'm going to be more comfortable here than I am back there in coach. Well, you can't sit here. All right, screw it, I'm not going to sit here and argue with you, I'll move. It was all really great for team unity.

That's one thing I did get changed with the Giants, at least temporarily. The thing I put across was that the press and the coaching staff and Wellington Mara and his friends ought to be moved up to first class with only football players in the back so you could sit and talk, do what you want, bitch if you want to, say anything you want and not have to worry about having somebody overhear you.

The whole bit was to get Wellington Mara away from the players so they could relax. Everybody voted for it and it passed. I think there were only two people who voted against it, good ol' Tucker Frederickson who wanted to sit up in first class and probably one of his friends who sat next to him. But that was it. Everybody else was for it. It worked fine the first trip but the second trip here comes Wellington right back in the middle of things again. You couldn't stop him. After all, he's Wellington Mara and he owns the club, therefore he pays for the plane, therefore he sits where he wants to sit. I made it clear that he was the one key person I didn't want back with the players but, you know, there's a song by Judy Collins that goes, "I stood for the Union and I fought in the line, fought against the company, now who's going to stand for me?" I found out who's going to stand for me, baby, ain't nobody, 'cause when I started getting in trouble I was all by myself out on the end of the plank.

Like my roommate Bruce Maher, who I respected as a man and a football player. His goal was to get in his ten years for the pension. We'd talk a lot about the problems and everything and he just said, You know, I agree with everything you're saying 100 per cent except for one thing, don't expect me to back you up. I can't afford to get in trouble, I've got a wife and family and the whole bit. I told him I had to try and if I got screwed I got screwed. I tried and I got screwed.

Bruce was right. If anybody backed me up, he'd only get in trouble, and I didn't want that. Bob

Lurtsema and I have always been friends and we used to help each other out as far as football was concerned, since he was a defensive tackle and we could exchange ideas. But Bob got benched, I'd say for associating with me. I'm not saying I know this for a fact but I know that he's a good football player and there was no reason for him to be benched. So I just stopped hanging around with him and I told him why. I said forget it, we can get together away from here. I felt bad about it, and I also had to wonder how the hell these people could play football with all this pettiness going on. The answer was, of course, they couldn't.

Even the practical jokers we had on the team tended to avoid me. Like Ralph Heck, one of the linebackers. He used to go around at training camp and wake everybody up about 10 o'clock at night and tell them there was a team meeting downstairs, then he'd go back to bed. But after a while, even he wouldn't mess with me. Finally, when I got suspended, only one player on the team called me, Lurtsema. It was just too dangerous to associate with me.

It got to the point that if anybody sought me out for advice or consolation or anything I just warned them they'd be better off staying away from me. I told a number of rookies, like Don Hermann, the wide receiver, Stay away from me kid, I'm trouble. You wanna stick around this team, don't mess with me. And they soon found out I was telling the truth.

I remember Rich Buzin because our lockers were next to each other and he'd always be talking to me. I'd say, Don't talk to me, Rich, I don't want to get you in trouble. One day he asks me something on the field about playing tackle and Rosey Brown was there and, as I said before, we didn't see eye to eye. Rosey got mad because Rich was talking to me and Rich, being a rookie and not knowing any better, said to Rosey, "I was just talking to my coach here," meaning me, and this just went over great. Like I said, I don't have to go looking for trouble, it just comes naturally.

To me, Tucker Frederickson was dead weight. You wanna talk about a star talk about Paul Hornung or Bart Starr or Jim Taylor, they're something. But to be constantly told how great this football player is and never see him play football gripes me. I guess the thing that really bugged me more than anything else was the attitude that, well, Tucker says it's so, so it must be so. Tucker gave the impression he was always thinking of himself as The Great Tucker Frederickson. Bobby Duhon for one worshipped the ground Tucker walked on. You know, it was like what do you want me to do now, Tucker? Sit up, roll over, lay down, play dead. It was just like a little boy following the big kid on the block. Eventually, he married Tucker's sister.

The big thing was the poker club on Monday night at Tucker's. Well, I don't gamble, so I didn't go. All right, so automatically it's like what's the matter with you? You can come anyway. For what? To sit around? I got other things I'd rather be doing. On other teams if you say you don't want to do something that's fine. On the Giants, uh-uh, there's gotta be a reason why.

Like, Come on down to Toots Shor's with us and drink. Well, for what, just to go down there and drink? I can drink in my own apartment. Well, we're all going down. Well, who all's going down? Well, you know, Tucker and Bobby Duhon and maybe Fran Tarkenton and Ernie Koy and Scott Eaton. Well, bullshit, who wants to spend the afternoon drinking at Toots Shor's?

Once I went over to another bar, P. J. Clarke's, with a friend and there was a line outside. We wanted to look for somebody inside but they wouldn't let us in. Just then I saw Tucker inside so I asked the maitre d', Would you go over there and tell Tucker Frederickson I'd like to see him for a second. I just wanted to walk in to see if I could find this friend. The guy came back and said, "Mr. Frederickson says he can't see you, he's busy right now." That's the way Tucker was.

I guess the only time I ever saw Tucker uptight was at one of his parties after a game. He had this big, round glass coffee table in his apartment and Tommy

Crutcher was getting bombed out of his mind. Somebody said something to him and he just got up with his shoes on and walked right across the top of Tucker's glass coffee table. I thought Tucker was going to faint on the spot. He had this look on his face like, He's not really walking across my coffee table, is he?

Crutcher did those kind of things. He was the linebacker who came with me in the trade from Green Bay, a big farm boy, one of ten kids, from McKinney, Texas, not even McKinney, outside of McKinney. It was nothing for him to be wandering the streets of New York at 5 o'clock in the morning barefoot, no shirt on, just a pair of pants, and it's about thirty degrees. Usually, he didn't know anything. Like what's your name? I don't know. Where you going? I don't know. Where'd you come from? I don't know. Once, he picked up some chick who was also walking the streets in the middle of the night. I think he had a hotel key with him from where he was staying and when he woke up the next day he didn't have a cent. She'd cleaned him out.

One time Crutcher had to make an appearance someplace in Connecticut and he was running late and had gotten lost. He was driving down one of these expressways with a cyclone fence in the middle. Well, Crutcher decided that he was going the wrong way and he had to turn around. Need I say more. Especially since he had a rented car. He saw a spot in the fence where somebody had hit it before and the fence was bent over maybe three feet off the ground and he figured if he hits it running fast enough he'll go right over it. So he hits it and the cyclone fence gets tangled up in the transmission and the car is stuck. No problem. He just left the car sitting there.

Crutcher and Koy shared Tucker's apartment, and Fran Tarkenton used one of the bedrooms when he felt like it since he was part of the married group that lived in upstate New York and was always commuting back and forth. They gave a lot of parties, and they could have them.

When I first got to New York I'd have parties, at least three times a week, in the afternoon, at night, anytime, and all of a sudden I realized I was going through an awful lot of booze and only a couple of guys, like Lurtsema and Mahar, were saying look here's a five, here's a ten. I wouldn't take it, though, because they're my kind of people, good tough football players who like to have a good time, nothing phony about them. But the rest of them, they'd come over and like maybe I started with two people and the next thing I knew there would be 15 up there and all drinking my booze and this goes on for a while and you realize, man, I'm going through $200 a week and these people aren't even my friends.

In fact, most of them wouldn't go out of their way for you in the least. Like at Thanksgiving, the Giants would give each of the players a turkey or ham, but I got busted up in a game out in Los Angeles right before Thanksgiving and spent three days in the hospital and two weeks flat on my back in my apartment after that, so I didn't get to pick mine up.

I didn't think anything about it, figuring they thought I didn't feel like eating anyway and gave it to somebody else. About a week later Bobby Duhon called me and said, "Listen, we picked up your turkey for you, you can come get it any time."

I lived at 520 E. 72d street and Duhon lived with Scott Eaton at 420 E. 72d, maybe 200 yards away. These are two of my teammates, they knew that I got busted up, they knew I spent time in the hospital, they knew I was stretched out because I hadn't been to practice and here they were 200 yards away with this turkey that's completely thawed out by now, sitting on some table and probably rotten, and it's like, you know, Come get your turkey when you want it.

This was typical behavior of the Giants. Another time I was supposed to make a personal appearance downtown with a linebacker named Ken Avery. He lived up on 84th Street, so he said he'd pick me up at about quarter of nine. We had to be there about 9:30. So I was out there on the street early just in case. Quarter of nine passed, then 9, then 9:15, then 9:30. I thought I'd better catch a cab. I got there about 10 o'clock. He never did show up. I saw him two days later and he said, Oh, yeah, I decided not to go. That was all there was to it.

Tucker and I got it off our chests during my first training camp with the Giants up at Fairfield, and Avery was involved in that too. I didn't like Tucker and he didn't like me, it was that simple. The thing came to a head one night when just about the whole team was out at a place nearby called the Surfside. I was talking to Avery. He was having his problems because the coaches were trying to change his style too.

He was telling me that all he wanted to do was go out there and hit people, and I was saying that's what you have to do if you're a defensive player. You let your emotions go so you really want to go in there and punish somebody. On offense you can't do this, there has to be some restraint and discipline. It takes a certain mental discipline to be an offensive player. On defense, you just read the play and go in there and knock the hell out of somebody. He was saying, Yeah, but they keep telling me this isn't what they want me to do. I'm saying, You're gonna have to play your game, you can't play it somebody else's way, I sure know that.

About this time Tarkenton came over and sat down and he was half-bombed, all of us were, and he started saying something about getting this team together, we gotta do this and we gotta do that. And I'm saying, Well okay that's beautiful, all you gotta do is get rid of these goddamn cliques around here. And he says there aren't any cliques on this team.

The position you love to hate; playing on the Green Bay special teams (I'm number 72) along with Ron Costelnik (77), Lionel Aldridge (82), and Tommy Joe Crutcher (37). VERNON J. BIEVER

Keeping a cool head as a Packer.
VERNON J. BIEVER

Giant coach Allie Sherman gives me a
little friendly advice. BILL MARK

I strike a heroic pose while sculptor
Daniel Schwartz molds the NFL's
Gladiator Award. GUY GILLETTE

Rosey Brown, my Giant line coach, seems to be directing most of his advice right at me. Judging by the expression on my face, I bet we weren't winning at the time. BILL MARK

Caught in the act of some minor felony.
Shucks, . . . Gee Whiz. I didn't mean it.

BILL MARK

Giant running back, Ron Johnson, and I
(78) don't have our timing down perfectly in this play against the Cardinals.
In fact, we don't even have it down a
little bit. BILL MARK

Taking my ease at the far end of the
Redskin bench with roomie Roy Schmidt.

NATE FINE

My favorite weapon: the smile.
RICHARD DARCEY

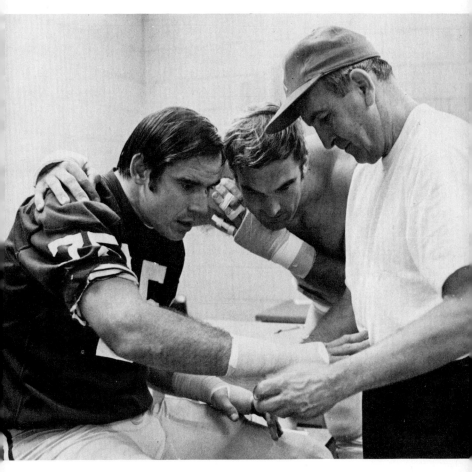

What is this bit? I look on with John
Hoffman as Redskin trainer Joe Kuczo
tapes my powerful wrists. NATE FINE

Mugging for the camera at a cocktail party with an amused Ricky Harris and a somewhat dazed Mike Bragg. We're all wearing name tags, just in case we get lost on the way home. NATE FINE

As a Cardinal (62) . . . . .

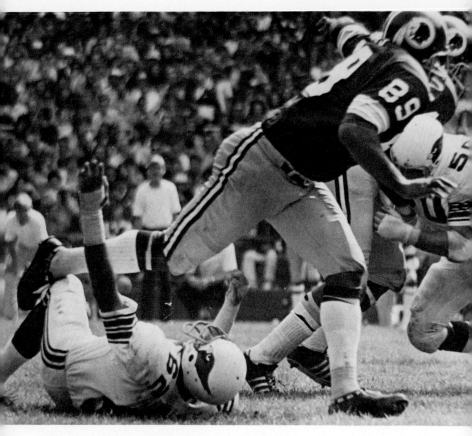

I try without notable success to block
Washington's Verlon Biggs . . . . .

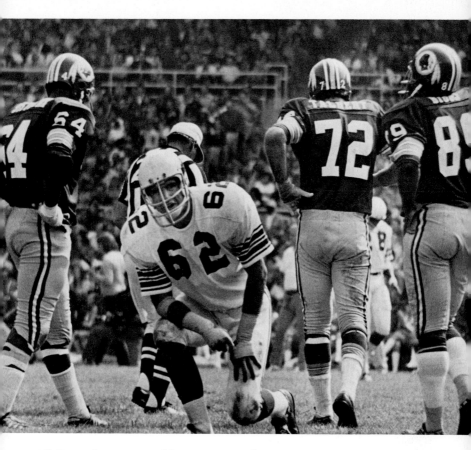

All I got for my trouble was injured.

RICHARD DARCEY

In my last NFL season, I still manage to look the part. RICHARD DARCEY

I said, Fran, who are you trying to kid? Look, every team has its cliques but the way they're set up around here they're tearing the team apart. It's one thing to have friends, one group can do what it wants to do, another group can do what it wants, but not when this group shuts this group out like they do with the Giants. And he was arguing all over the place that there weren't any cliques, and I'm saying, Don't be an ass, you know there are cliques and they're tearing the team apart and everybody else knows it too.

So he got pissed off and left and I went back to talking to Avery about how he should be playing. But apparently Fran said something to Tucker about me mentioning cliques so Tucker comes over and says, "Get outta here, Wright, what are you talking to this kid about?" And I'm saying, Hey, nobody asked you over here. I'm sitting here talking to Ken, nobody said a word to you about anything. He said, "I heard what you were saying, you were talking about cliques and that I'm bad for this club." I said, I didn't say that, I don't think I mentioned your name, and besides we were talking about something else. Hey, Ken, tell Tucker what we were talking about.

Ready for this? Avery says, "We were talking about cliques."

Okay, that's it. I mean that was the whole scene on the Giants. That's why nobody trusted anybody. This is what was tearing that team apart, little digs among the players. Like I was trying to help the kid, trying to be nice, and he says, in effect, fuck you, I've got to stay in good with this guy. You know, you get kicked in the teeth so many times you just finally say fuck 'em all.

I wasn't always up to my neck in shit with the Giants. Believe it or not, they once selected me to represent them on a goodwill trip to the Far East. It was after the 1968 season, I'd had a good year until I got hurt. I even posed as the model for a statue called The Gladiator, which is given as the NFL Man of the Year award. A New York artist named Daniel Schwartz sculptured the figure of me in uniform with a cape around my shoulders.

The award goes to the "outstanding citizen-athlete" in the league every season. The statue is supposed to represent the ideal football player, a composite of every man who ever played, or will ever play, professional football. I read somewhere that the word *gladiator* "evokes a mental picture of strength, quality, victory."

Boy, they sure picked a bummer to pose for it, didn't they? The guys who won would turn over in their graves if they knew it was me. Bart Starr, Johnny Unitas, John Hadl, Willie Lanier. They all won a statue of me.

The Giants' publicity department went wild over me after that first season. The press guide for the following year said, "One of the best trades the Giants made in recent years was the deal that brought tackle Steve Wright (plus linebacker Tommy Joe Crutcher) from the Green Bay Packers. Wright was a tower of strength," and so on. You better believe none of that stuff appeared in the 1970 book.

So off I went on this trip, with Namath, Marv Fleming from Green Bay, Jim Otto from Oakland, and a sportscaster, Charlie Jones. We went for a month and visited military hospitals in Japan, Okinawa, the Philippines, and Hawaii.

Namath was something on that trip. One night we were all sitting in a little restaurant in Tokyo and Jim Otto is just driving this waiter crazy. He knows we're somebody but he can't figure out what the scene is. None of us knows Japanese and Jim keeps going, "Hi, hi, hi," and the waiter is going around in circles because he doesn't know what Jim wants.

So the waiter walks over to Joe—this whole conversation is half in sign language—and he asks, Are you a movie star, and Joe says, Yeah. He said, What's your name. Joe says Clark Gable. No. Yeah. Really? Yeah. Can I have your autograph? So Joe writes down Clark Gable and gives it to him. This waiter runs back and all of a sudden he's surrounded by about three chefs, fifteen waiters, and two maitre d's, and half of them are shaking their heads no and the other half are going, Yeah, that's really him over there.

When I got back, the problems on the Giants got

worse, and it was all so petty. The trouble that eventually led to my suspension started during the exhibition season. I hadn't signed my contract and I had a knee busted up and a groin muscle that was still messed up from the previous season, but the other tackles were hurt, and they wanted me to play. I said I didn't want to play in an exhibition game with a bad knee if I didn't have a signed contract. They were in a bind, they needed me at the time, and it didn't matter that I was hurting, they wanted me in there.

We had lost our first four exhibitions, and things were getting tense. This was our last one and, as it turned out, Allie's last game. So Tim Mara, Well's nephew, negotiated with me. I asked him for $25,000 and he said they couldn't go for it. I told him I wasn't about to play with a knee that was maybe 75 percent okay, go out there and really get busted up. With no contract, I'd have nothing.

He said the doctor said I was all right. I'm saying, Yeah, okay, the doctor's not walking on my knee either. Oh, the doctor was great. I had gone in to see him the day before and he grabs hold of my knee and he kind of bends it back and forth and he pushes here and there and he says, "Does it hurt there?" And I say, Yeah. He says, "Oh, good, then you're all right." You gotta be kidding me.

Tim's second offer was my previous season's contract, $20,000, with a $5,000 bonus if I made the starting team. I was starting right tackle at the time so

I figured that's fine with me. It turned out I started one game all season. One game, that's all. I never got the $5,000.

So we flew up to Montreal to play Pittsburgh, and it was a horrible game and, sure enough, I hurt my knee even worse and what really made me mad was that it happened when I was playing out of position, at left tackle. We lost, 17-13, and it was a Thursday night and the stadium was practically empty. The crowd was announced as 12,000-something but it was more like 8,000, if that. And the people were chanting, Good-by Allie in French, "Bon soir, Allie."

When we got back to the locker room, everybody started ranting and raving, screaming at everybody else, and they wanted to hold a team meeting right there after the game, so they asked all the coaches and Wellington Mara to leave.

I started it off. I got up and said how really stupid it was for a team with so much talent to be so uptight about one person, this person being Well Mara. I said, Nobody can be a man on the field if he isn't a man off the field, that everybody ought to be able to relax wherever he is.

Then I said, It's really ridiculous when you're afraid to say "fuck" in the locker room because somebody might be standing behind you and you might lose your job for saying it.

And with this, Fran just goes berserk. He jumps up

and says, "That's right, God damn it, if you want to say 'fuck' say fuck. Fuck, fuck, fuck." It was hysterical.

Then he gives a spiel like, We're all men here and we're sick and tired of losing these games and everybody being afraid of who's standing behind you or who's sitting in front of you or anything else. We've got a good football team and by God you ought to be able to say what you want to say. Don't you all agree? And everybody chimes in, Yeah, yeah.

But, really, watching Fran get emotional is like watching a Looney-Tunes cartoon. He just isn't convincing. I mean, it was ridiculous. He was slamming stuff down and kicking stuff around. Come on, Fran, get outta here with the kid stuff. Yet he probably convinced some of them. To me, he was just politicking. It seemed like the time for him to get up and say something, so he did.

I couldn't resist a small joke when we were getting on the bus, so as I walked past Wellington, knowing how small the crowd has been, I said, Did we break even? You know, we lost the game, might as well find out if we made any money on it at least, what the hell. But he didn't dig it.

He was in a lousy mood. The next morning he fired Allie.

Surprisingly enough, Allie was a good football coach, as far as strategy and tactics were concerned. He just didn't handle people very well. I found out about that with the bit about not getting nervous but if you don't play better I'm gonna trade you on the spot. Allie was a beauty dealing with people, a real piece of work.

I think his smallness and slight build were a hangup with him. It was common knowledge that if Allie got mad at you and started chewing you out you could stand your ground and back him into a wall. Everybody knew that so it cost him respect from the players. They stepped on his inferiority complex, and this was his biggest problem.

Another thing, he apparently didn't realize how serious the cliques were. Alex Webster did. When he took over as coach after Allie was fired, he got his message across. His approach was, I don't care what the hell you people do, I don't care if you love each other or hate each other's guts, you better play on Sunday and on the practice field. Once you leave here I could care less what you do, but if I catch you not putting out on the field I'll get rid of you. It's that simple.

Training camp under Alex was less of a strain because there wasn't any nitpicking. He knew we were going to sneak out. He had been a ballplayer, he knew. His feeling was, and this is also one of my contentions, that I'm not going to try to catch you. I'm not going to come sneaking around, looking around corners, which is what the whole New York Giant scene was. But if I catch you, I'm going to bust you. And if I don't catch you, you just better be able to do a good day's work the next day.

With Allie, they used to have one check, two checks, three checks a night, stuff like that. You never really knew when they would be. I sneaked out anyway. One time, it was a bummer. A couple of us were supposed to meet some girls at a bar. When we got there, the girls weren't there, and by the time we got back, about 12:30, it was pouring rain. We parked the car, then we decided we shouldn't go in the front door and make all kinds of noise, so we took off our shoes and went running across the lawn and sneaking up the outside stairway. We got up to the second floor and we're walking down the hall when I turned around and saw a couple of size ten and size eleven footprints behind us—and then I see a gigantic size fifteen. Could there be any doubt who that was? I could just imagine one of the assistants coming up and saying, Allie wants to see you. But it never happened.

One night they got my roommate, Bruce Maher. He was always somewhere except the room, either playing cards or bullshitting in another room, he was never where he was supposed to be. Only this time he had a legitimate reason. One of his kids was sick and he was up on the third floor making calls back and forth to his home in Michigan. So about 12:30 one of the coaches, I think it was Ken Kavanaugh, came in. "Where's Bruce? Not here? Okay, tell him to come down and see me when he gets back."

I guess it was about 1:30 and Bruce had to go down and tell the coaches like a little kid where he had been, and for Bruce Maher, one of the toughest little defensive backs in the league, to do that is like me trying to tell something straight without making a joke of it. When he walked in, the whole coaching staff was there, and Wellington, too. When he came back, he said, "First time in my life I told the truth and nobody believed me."

That's how it was under Allie, kid stuff. One time, at camp, he decided to really put on the whole bag for us. He got the hall at Fairfield University and he hired a band and a couple of acts, a magician yet. Beautiful. You're all going to have a good time and that's an order. Here they have a six-piece band playing and not a chick in the place. Here are forty guys sitting there going, Oh boy, wow, come on honey, you wanna dance. It was "Stalag 17" all over again.

There was no way there could be a girl around, that wouldn't be locking in, would it? Pete Gent came up to training camp with a girl he since married, and immediately he was guilty of not locking in. She stayed at a motel nearby, and one day she was sitting in the stands and she had on a see-through blouse and the cops ran her out. This just wasn't the proper thing to do, according to the Giants, and I have to believe that his bringing along a girl friend had something to do with getting him cut. I talked to him when it happened and he was saying Wellington gave him the

103

line like Pete, We think you're one of our best receivers. We've been watching you and you're doing fantastic. But we're gonna cut you anyway. This was typical New York bullshit.

We really did lock in before the first Giants-Jets game, the exhibition in the Yale Bowl. The Jets had waited for this for years. And Wellington had kept them waiting. The Giants had not only refused to play the Jets, they wouldn't admit the Jets existed. But when they finally played, the Jets were the world champions. The only thing I could think about was, Here we go for the city championship. Next year maybe we'll go for the state. The only thing was everybody else on the Giants was very uptight.

We were in camp and everybody was told not to say a single word. Allie says, "If I see anything in the paper, I'll cut you. I'll trade you in a minute if you say one word to the newspapers. Don't give 'em a thing to work on. It's just another football game. We're gonna lock in and we're not gonna cop out."

So if a reporter or anybody talked to a Giant the player would say, "It's just another game. It's just an exhibition. We're not going to do anything differently."

Meanwhile, the Jets were saying, "We'll kill the sons of bitches. We're going to annihilate them. We'll eat 'em up and spit 'em out. Boy, are we waiting for the Giants."

So we finally got up there and we did get annihilated, 37-14, and it could have been worse. The next Tuesday we're sitting there waiting to look at the films and waiting for the worst kind of ass-chewing when Allie comes up with the most fantastic explanation of what happened.

"All right, you guys, we got beat, and you know why we got beat? I'll show you why. Turn on the projector. Look at that, you see that? Everybody's standing up on the sidelines. That's why we got beat. Look at their bench. They're all sitting down.

"We're all standing up. No organization on our bench. Nobody knows what's going on. Look at them. Everybody's on the bench, in the right spot."

Gospel. He was dead serious. We lost the game because we stood up on the sideline. And where was I? Standing up on the sideline the whole game, disorganizing everyone, I guess. I had a groin injury and didn't play at all.

Allie also said, "Incidentially, Wellington Mara says he's never been so hurt in all his life." Sniff, sniff, it made tears come to your eyes. Half the coaches put in their resignations, but they weren't accepted. And this was the team that said it was just another game.

I remember coming back to New York on the team bus after the game and somebody handed me a warm six-pack but I didn't have an opener. So I borrowed Allie's pen knife.

That night Bruce Maher and I went over to

Bachelor's III to see Joe and congratulate him, kind of a visit to the enemy camp. I don't know if word of that ever got back or not.

Before his last season, Allie sent us all a bunch of postcards as part of an off-season conditioning program he concocted. The whole bit was to run twice a week as far as you could in twelve minutes without stopping and send in the postcards telling how far you got. Hell, I've got fifteen million things on my mind besides sending in those goddamn postcards. And then I was sent a letter saying they wanted me to report at 245 pounds. But I was working out and I felt good so I came in at 250. But they fined me $500 because I came in five pounds over and they said they were also fining me $50 for each postcard I hadn't sent in.

Well, when I unpacked I found a bunch of the postcards so I just signed, Sincerely, Steve Wright, Sincerely, Steve Wright, on all of them, and handed them in. There must have been about fifteen or twenty, and I said, You wanted them, here they are. You didn't say there was any time limit or anything. If you wanna break chops, I can break chops, too. We can even take it to court. So they only got me for three of them, which I must have lost.

It was all nonsense. One guy who recognized it for what it was was Homer Jones, but nobody took Homer seriously. His image as a character had already been established and embellished by the Giants' publicity department. You know, Homer read comic books. Homer had trouble running a fly pattern, which is a straight line. Homer didn't know anything about Vietnam or world affairs. Homer lived in his own little world.

Nobody really knew how old Homer was, that was another thing. Apparently all his birth records were burned up in a fire in the little town where he came from Pittsburg, Texas. I think when he reached thirty he started counting backwards.

Anyway, one story about him became legend. He was asked if a transit strike that was going on would keep him from getting to practice, and he supposedly answered, "Naw, I take the subway."

This one, though, I heard myself. Homer had bought a new boat, I guess about a sixteen or eighteen-foot fiber glass job with about a hundred horsepower outboard, and he was going around telling everybody how fast it would go, like it'd go sixty miles an hour and pull four skiers. And one of the players asked him if he water skied and Homer says, No, I don't water ski, I can't even swim. If I could swim why would I need a boat? That was Homer.

If Homer wasn't an intellectual giant, he at least was a good football player. He knew what had to be done to win. He would have fit in at Green Bay. At Green Bay, everybody knew what had to be done. Like Hornung would get up and say, Everybody knows what we have to do, we just have to go out there and hit and that's it. It was that simple. When you're dealing with men who are professionals, not people who play professionally but people who are real professionals, nothing really need be said.

Whereas on the Giants, no one really knew what the hell to do to start with. Nobody could inspire anybody. It was a beautiful scene to watch some of these team meetings the Giants were always calling. It was like, Who's gonna do it first? Not me, uh-uh, I'm not gonna say anything first, you say it first. You go. No, you go. No, you go.

There was one when Allie called the whole team together and everybody had something to say at once. I think Pete Case got up and he started screaming. And then Fran started screaming. But as usual he just wasn't convincing, no way, it really didn't cut it.

But when Homer got up he says, You can sit there and you can talk about all kinds of things all day long but it all comes down to one thing: you've got to do it on the field. It was that simple, yet nobody on the Giants could understand that. They were too busy thinking about what was going on off the field. They never paid much attention to Homer, yet Homer actually had some pretty good philosophy. I think they took him as a buffoon, but he wasn't. In his own way, he was a hell of a football player, and he said what he thought.

Hardly anybody else did, though. After one game,

when we got back in the locker room, Greg Larson throws his helmet down on the floor, jumps up and says, "All right, goddamn it, I'm sick and tired . . . Oh, excuse me, Father. I didn't see you standing there." It was Father Dudley, the priest who traveled with us, the chaplain of the Giants. This was the whole scene at New York, everybody was afraid of his own shadow because you might say something wrong around one of Wellington's friends.

But for Larson to have to say, "Oh, excuse me, Father, I didn't see you there" is to blow the whole scene. You've got to say it the way you feel it. I'm not gonna say, Oh, excuse me, I beg your pardon, now what was I gonna say, well heck, gosh darn it all, because that wouldn't be my immediate feeling and nobody would listen to me. But I'd keep my job.

Bruce Maher used to use the language of the moment, and he was told a number of times by players to watch his language, to be careful. But he always said things the way he felt them, and he was asked not to report back after the 1969 season.

It just wasn't a professional operation. Wellington's friends were always around, businessmen, associates, even kids—Wellington's kids. His kids would play Ping-Pong and chase each other and play tag all through the locker room the day of the game. A half-hour before the game, they'd be chasing each other and throwing chalk back and forth at each other. It was unreal.

109

At training camp, Wellington would be out there walking around with a little notebook, jotting down notes. I don't know what he was writing down but if he looked at you you just moved around a little bit to make him think you were doing something because he wouldn't know the difference anyway.

It was a frightening atmosphere to be involved in. I remember when we went up to Minnesota for a game I took along a tape recorder. I usually go down to the locker room early to get taped so I set up the recorder and put on some music, just relaxing before the game. But in walks Allie and says, What are you doing with that? I said, I'm listening to the music, which seemed like a reasonable answer. "We didn't come here to listen to music. Turn that thing off." Here I was right back at Alabama. Nobody had complained about the music. Nobody had protested. Who was it hurting? But again, this was life on the Giants. You never knew what you could do or couldn't do until you were told you'd done something wrong, and then you were in trouble.

It was grim. And the closer Allie came to being fired the longer the practices became, like an hour and a half longer. I used to give three cheers out there like, Let's set a record, let's go for an all-timer and make it three hours today. Talk about tension, whew. By this time, Allie was as much of a problem as Well.

When Alex took over, he was more relaxed. He was

liked by the guys because he had played football for the Giants and was one of their all-time greats. He just wanted you to play football and that was it. But he wasn't a head coach, or at least not my interpretation of a head coach. My idea of a head coach is one who takes command, decides what to do, then delegates the jobs to his assistants, and it was just the reverse with Alex. The assistants did the planning and they funneled their ideas through Alex. He was more of a cheerleader, a figurehead. He would get up in front and say, Okay we gotta do this or we gotta do that, or, I'm proud of you guys, or, I'm pissed at you guys, and then the rest of the coaches would take over. Maybe this was because he took over the team the week before the season opened and didn't have a chance to change things.

I spent more time sitting in the stands watching the games in 1969 than I did playing in them. I watched four of them from up in the seats when I was injured because, get this, there wasn't enough room for me on the bench. I was told there were too many people out there, almost all of them happening to be friends of Wellington Mara's. I was only on the team.

One Sunday I walked into the dressing room before a game and asked one of the front office people for a sideline pass, never imagining there'd be any problem. He says, "We've got an awful lot of people on the sideline now, we don't have any more passes." He didn't even say he was sorry, just "There's too many people on the bench, we can't let anybody else down there." I'm saying, Wait a minute, I play for this team, remember. Uh-uh, it didn't matter. So I ended up using my season ticket seats.

After that I said something about what happened to Spider Lockhart, one of the captains, that it's really something when the players don't have seats on the sideline but friends of Wellington Mara do. So Spider went to Alex and Alex asked me about it and I said, Yeah, that was right, and he says, Okay, we'll straighten it out. The next week exactly the same thing happened, so I'm saying to myself, Uh-huh, they're trying to tell me something.

I learned one thing in the stands. The seats are terrible for football in Yankee Stadium. I can sympathize with the fans from first-hand experience, and how many players can say that? I was about three-quarters of the way up in the third deck. It was awful.

Worse than that, it kills you being up there, it tears your guts out. I wanted to be playing, to be part of the team. But I didn't let on, I just sat up there and joked about it. Somebody would come along and say, "Hey, there's Steve Wright," or "Hey, Steve, how come you're sitting up here?" I'd say, Figured I'd do more good up here than down there. It was strange, I'd leave maybe five minutes early, ahead of the crowd, and go down to the locker room and wait for the guys to come in. It was just personal pride. I wanted the team to know I was there, even though most of them didn't give a damn about me.

I got an inkling of what was going to happen because of an incident with Rosey Brown. It was the second game in Detroit. I had started the first one and gotten banged up, so I was on the sidelines wearing street clothes. Suddenly Rosey comes up out of nowhere and accuses me of disrupting the team and says, "Don't talk to any of the guys." I said, Okay, I can take a hint. The Giants were shut out that day and I guess I was a handy guy to take it out on.

This goes on for a couple more games. I'm not playing, I'm on the inactive list, so one Friday, before a Monday night game in Dallas, I went up to Alex and asked him if he was planning to activate me. He said he didn't know yet. I asked him when he would know. He said, "I don't know, why?"

I told him, "My daughter's birthday is this weekend and I'd like to see her in Green Bay on her birthday."

He says, "As it stands now, no, we're not going to activate you."

I said, "All right, then I'm going to take off to Green Bay."

He said, "All right."

So I took off. I get back on Tuesday and the first thing I hear is that the Giants lost the game and I'm fined $750. For what? Spider asked me where I was and I told him the whole story. Then I went to see Alex.

He says, "Where were you?"

I said, "What do you mean where was I? I told you I was going to Green Bay."

"Yeah, but I didn't think you were leaving then."

"I told you I was."

"You just can't take off like that. What would have happened if somebody had gotten hurt?"

"That's why I asked."

"I don't want to talk about it anymore." That was it. It cost me $750.

The Giants were floundering in the middle of a seven-game losing streak when I was finally activated. We were in St. Louis and the Cardinals were beating the hell out of us, 42-17, and I was sitting on the bench next to Spider Lockhart. It's the fourth quarter and it's getting worse and worse and we're trying to avoid everybody. All of a sudden I hear my name called with only a couple of minutes to go and it's Rosey Brown saying, "Go on in." I'm saying to him, Naw, you're kidding me. He says, "No, go ahead in." So I turn around and look at Spider and he just has this big grin on his face like, They gotcha.

So I'm standing there putting on my helmet and thinking lot of good this is going to do. As I'm walking by Alex I can see him looking at me out of the corner of his eye so I said, "What do you want me to do, Coach, win it or just tie it up?" I don't think he heard me and it's just as well.

November 19, 1969, a day of infamy that'll never be forgotten, by Steve Wright anyway. I walked in that morning and my locker was cleaned out. You think Mother Hubbard's cupboard was bare, you should have seen my locker. So I started looking for somebody and there wasn't anybody around. Finally, I found Alex and he said, "I want to talk to you," and then he let me have it. He said I had been "suspended indefinitely for conduct detrimental to the Giants and to professional foorball."

My first reaction was, What did I do? I honestly didn't know.

"I don't want to talk about it," he said.

"You're suspending me indefinitely from the National Football League and you don't want to talk about it, you don't want to tell me why?"

"I told you I don't want to talk about it."

By that time I was so mad I had tears in my eyes and I was ready to go at it with Alex right there. But for some reason—I'm glad whatever it was—I just turned around and walked out.

Suspended. But why? My name was being blackened all over the place and I didn't even know what the reason was. All kinds of fantastic rumors were circulating, all of them untrue. They had me throwing my helmet through a window, throwing matches at people in the locker room, even smoking under my helmet on the field, can you believe that? A friend of mine called from Milwaukee and said the reporters out there were saying I had gotten into a fist fight and had punched out Alex. Incredible.

Another thing that was mentioned in the papers as a reason for the suspension was that I'd disassociated myself from the rest of the team because I sat in the back of the room during team meetings. But what wasn't mentioned was that Fran Tarkenton sat back there, too, no more than two or three feet away from me. But because I was in the back of the room I was a loner and was trying to start trouble.

I sat back there for a simple reason. It was more comfortable. I could prop my feet up on another chair if I wanted to. And there was a trash box in the back that I could flip my cigarette butts into.

Well, it was two weeks before I found out why I was suspended and, sure enough, there really wasn't any reason for it. It all stemmed from one of those team meetings. We were sitting in there—we had lost five straight so, again, somebody's got to take some shit—and Alex starts talking about people with bad attitudes.

"You're one, Wright. You really think you're King Shit, don't you? You don't really care what happens to the New York Giants, do you?"

I said, "No, that's not right."

But Wellington only heard me say No, naturally.

He didn't hear the rest of the sentence, or at least he said he didn't. And that's why I was suspended—because Wellington said I said I didn't care what happened to the New York Giants.

Two weeks later I had a meeting with Wellington, at his request, in the training room and he starts telling me he doesn't understand this and he doesn't understand that and he doesn't understand why my attitude is like it is. Then he tells me that Rosey Grier used to lay down in meetings and sleep. I said, "Hey, I never fell asleep in a meeting." He says, "No, but you know what I mean." I said, "No, tell me what you mean."

He said, "Didn't you say you didn't care what happened to the Giants?"

"No," I said, "I never said that in my life and I never would."

"I heard you say it," he said.

"I don't know what you heard but I know what I said and there are other people who heard what I said, too."

But those people never came up and said what they heard, except to me privately. Tarkenton never said anything. He sat only a couple of feet away, he heard what I said, but I never heard a word from him.

Alex told me later he had heard me answer something but didn't know exactly what and didn't think any more about it. And that Wellington had come up to him after the meeting and said, "Did you hear what Wright said? He said he didn't care what happened to the New York Giants." Wouldn't you know it, I got suspended solely because of Wellington.

Before I found that out, when I was waiting and wondering and nobody would tell me anything, I finally decided I was gonna stick it in their ear. So I called a press conference at Mr. Laff's, an appropriate place, I think, to tell my side of the story.

A number of things fell into place before the press conference. I met with Wellington. Then I met with the players' committee and they told me I was going to be reinstated.

So, by accident, it turned out to be sort of a counter press conference. I scooped the Giants. I came out the day before Wellington and announced that I was being reinstated, and this blew his mind again.

Actually, the Giants violated the player contract because they're supposed to go through a player committee before they suspend somebody. But Wellington had the player committee in one hip pocket and the coach in the other.

I found out that as a professional football player the owners can do anything they want to me. They can suspend me for looking cross-eyed if they want to. I have no say in the matter. Wellington just decided he wanted to get rid of me—and he did, even though it took until the following summer because of the good press I received during the suspension.

I may have been reinstated, but I was never

reactivated. I never played another game for the Giants.

I expected to get cut from the first day I walked into training camp the following summer. I found out right off that I was the second team left tackle. I hardly ever played left tackle before, only in emergencies at Green Bay. I'd been the starting right tackle for the Giants, now all of a sudden I was the second team left tackle. Let's say I could see the handwriting on the wall.

They wanted to get rid of me and this was their way of doing it. They thought they'd done it the year before with the suspension but I fooled 'em. So they waited the whole off-season. I was hoping they'd trade me, maybe to the Jets, and I called up Alex and asked him if I was going to be back or if he would trade me. Oh no, he said he wanted to let bygones be bygones and I'm saying to myself, Okay, whatever Wellington tells you to say is fine with me.

But when I reported to training camp no one wanted to have anything to do with me. It was like, Hey, Wright, you stand over there, we've got work to do over here. So I said the hell with it.

There were a few laughs during the last days, thanks to Freddie Dryer. Freddie's something like me. He's the kind of guy who just doesn't give a damn about anything, they had so much money invested in him and he's such a good football player they had to put up with him.

Freddie can do the most fantastic imitations of Wellington Mara you ever heard in your life. Wellington is definitely not a dapper guy and he talks kind of tight-lipped. I'd say he could be mistaken for an encyclopedia salesman. Freddie likes to do Wellington Mara talking to Jim Trimble, which is like Alphonse talking to Gaston. Trimble is another one of the biggies. One of his jobs, and I have to laugh at this, was "liaison" between Wellington and Alex, as if Wellington was ever more than a few feet away.

Freddie plays both parts, first Wellington, then Trimble, and it goes for about fifteen minutes and neither guy is really saying anything, just gibberish. It's great late at night at training camp in somebody's room. With the door locked. Freddie may be a little wacko, but he's not stupid.

I do W.C. Fields imitations myself, and I guess I should have done them in private, too, but I couldn't resist. I have to admit I did them right out there on the bench during the games, but some of those games were so bad you had to do something to break the monotony. So every once in a while I'd say something like, There we go again, another fantastic play, three yards and a cloud of dust. It'd get a lot of laughs, probably too many.

But what I think disturbed the Giants more than that was where I was sitting, at the very end of the bench. I mean, it's against the rules. You're supposed to sit in a particular spot. Say the offensive line sits in one place and the defensive line sits in another, very orderly.

The problem is when I come off the field I hate to be looking around for a place to sit down and nine times out of ten there's a spot at the end of the bench. That's why I sit there.

Hell, I even got in trouble on my very last day with the Giants. It was ironic. I slept through breakfast the morning I got cut. I didn't do it intentionally, I did it inadvertently, like a lot of things I do.

A kid came up to me that morning and said Alex wanted to see me in his office. And like that's the scene right there. You know what he wants. So I got this big grin on my face and went to see him. He told me they hadn't had a chance to look at me since camp started late because of the players' strike, that he didn't know if I could play football or not, and that he was just going to have to let me go.

I said, Alex, who are you trying to kid? This isn't some rookie you're talking to. He said, "You know what the situation is." I said, Yeah, I know. I've been expecting this since the first day. How come it took you this long?

Then I got serious for a minute, I guess because I wanted him to know I cared. I told him, The one thing this team needs is a leader. That's all it needs, somebody to pull it together and make a team out of it because all it is now is a bunch of guys out on a field playing football.

After I cleaned out my room, I got on my motorcycle, a Triumph 650 Bonneville, and I rode down to the locker room to pick up my shoes. Everybody was out on the practice field and I sure wasn't going to leave with my head hung down. That wouldn't be me. So I just waved to evervbody as I rode past, like Yoo hoo, so long. and rolled on out of there.

I wasn't worried because I knew I was gonna play somewhere. One of the reporters asked me what my plans were and I said my immediate intention was to go back to my apartment and pour myself a big Chivas Regal and water and then I added, It only costs a little more to go first class.

Some New York liquor company read that in the paper and sent me over a couple of fifths of Chivas Regal with a note that said, "The New York Giants' loss is our gain. Anybody who goes as first class as you deserves our appreciation."

We had some party that night. By six o'clock there were about fifteen people in my apartment just having a ball. I put on a caftan with a hood that I had bought for some unknown reason, and sandals, and I was set.

The party floated around between my place and a bar around the corner called Sugar Man's and at one point I think I remember sort of a parade down the street, one guy carrying part of an awning and everybody else with some other pieces of junk.

I guess it was the next day when the phone rang

122

and it was Tim Temerario of the Redskins' front office and he was saying, "Hey, where've you been?" And I said to myself, Oh, boy, here we go again.

WASHINGTON

My first impression of the Washington Redskins was, Just another football team, and it went downhill from there. I wasn't overwhelmed, to say the least. It had to be the ideal club for Washington. Half of the guys should have been in politics instead of football, they had to be talking a good game to still be playing.

When I first got to Washington, Vince Lombardi had been the coach for a year, and his philosophies and ideals and everything were still very apparent. But after he died the whole thing just went right down the drain. It took about three weeks for the team to finally realize that Vince wasn't there any-more and everyone could go back to being the Wash-ington Redskins they were before he came. Every-body ran around like a bunch of chickens with their heads cut off. It just folded up, a dead team.

The Redskins were a paradox because, like the Giants, they had some good football players yet there was no real team. On the Giants there was a reason for it, at Washington there wasn't. The word for the situation was "vacuum." Nobody really gave a shit about anybody else. You sit down and try and figure out why that is, and there's no reason, yet nobody was gonna take the initiative to try and change things, least of all me. If you don't learn from your past mistakes, you deserve to be kicked in the face a second time. So I was just gonna sit there on the bench and wave my Redskins pennant, Go team, Go.

Now that I was finding out what it's like to play for the average football team, screw it, just pay me. I tried with the Giants to do what I thought was right and got kicked in the teeth for it. Uh-uh, never again. Just give me the paycheck, I'm a mercenary now. And that's what I knew I'd continue to be unless something or somebody could get me excited about football again, unless I found a team that really wanted to play. I looked, but I never found anything.

I didn't play regularly with the Redskins until the next to the last game, when Walter Rock, the starting right tackle, got hurt and they had to carry him off

126

the field. The only game I started was the very last one. After that, Bill Austin, who had taken over as coach after Vince died, said something like, I should have been starting you all year. Well, that wasn't going to do me a damn bit of good at the end of the season.

I never talked to Austin about not playing. I had the attitude, I'm here, if you want to play me, play me. Really, I could sympathize with Austin, being kind of an interim coach put him in an awkward situation. He was presented with the team Vince had picked, it had been winning exhibition games, so why take a chance? He was afraid to change things, put in any innovations. He had a set system, why mess it up?

If I was younger, and more eager, I might have asked why I wasn't playing. But let's face it, I'm a football player, so I want to play football. You're paying me, you want a job done, I'll do it, and I'll do it the best I can, and that's it.

But I'm not going to start waving my own flag or try to cut somebody's throat. And I'm not going looking for compliments. Very few things make me nervous, but the hardest thing for me to accept is a sincere compliment from someone.

You know, you watch the films, you see what's going on out there, and it's demoralizing. Do you want somebody who can block, or do you want somebody who's a nice guy who's gonna do a half-assed job? I really felt sorry for our running backs, players like Larry Brown and Charley Harraway. They did eighty per cent of their own blocking. With the exception of maybe a couple of players, I don't see how our offensive and defensive lines were in the NFL, I really don't. This is why I couldn't really get myself excited, why I sat on the bench like I could give a shit less.

In team meetings I'd sit with Roy Schmidt, who'd been at Green Bay too, and who knew what a professional team is supposed to be like. We'd watch the films, and we'd see somebody block, just make a lousy block, and the comment from one of the coaches would be, Did you see that? Yeah, coach. Well, you're blocking with your head down, aren't you? Yeah, coach. See that next block, what did you do wrong there? I'm blocking with my head down again, coach. That's right, and what are you gonna do about it? I'm gonna change, coach, I'm gonna block with my head up. That's right, so you can see where you're going, right? Right.

I mean, where are we, are we starting all over from the beginning now or what? I mean, if you don't even know how to block, what are you doing in the pros? I looked at Roy and I said, All you gotta do around this place is block with your head down, at least then they know you're around.

So then it was at the stage with me where I just didn't care. If you want me around, fine, if you don't want me around, fine, I could care less, it doesn't make any difference to me. I didn't feel that I owed any extra allegiance to the Washington Redskins. It's not, This is my team, right or wrong. That's all bullshit. I've changed my mind about the old adage, Just keep going whether you're hurt or not. Now it's, I'm hurt, Coach, take me out, I've got my hand up.

It was a Thursday, the very last day of the Redskins' Carlisle, Pa., camp when I arrived, and there was to be an exhibition game with the Buffalo Bills in Washington the following night. That turned out to be funny, because I obviously didn't know any of the guys on the team and, while some clubs use colors as signals for different types of blocks, the Redskins wanted you to call out the names of your buddies.

There was one play where I was supposed to exchange blocks with the tight end, who at the time was Gary Beban, the Heisman Trophy winner who never made it. I could see the position of the Buffalo man and I knew that I was going to take him, and I was supposed to tell Beban by calling out his name, Beban. But I didn't know who the hell he was, so I just yelled out I'll take him, like it was some pickup game. I mean what the hell, might as well let him know. But sure enough, we both blocked the same guy, and there was one man who wasn't blocked and he made the tackle. I collided with Beban and he says like, What happened? And I said, I don't know, and by the way, what's your name?

I guess you could say my reputation preceded me to the Redskins. One of the comments I got on my first day from Bill Austin, the head coach, was, "This is not the New York Giants here, we want good serious football players, we don't want comedians." And I said, Hey, that's all I wanna do, play football. Me, a troublemaker? Not a bit.

I don't know if he believed me or not, but the Redskins never did trust me with a playbook. Everyone had one but me, although I didn't need one, really. Most of the plays were familiar from Green Bay. We got a sheet with them written on it every Tuesday in preparation for Sunday's game, and we went over them every day in practice, so if you've been around you can do without a book.

At the end of the year one of the assistant coaches collected all the offensive linemen's books, and he looked at me and said, "Did I get yours?" I said, No, I tried to sell it to five different teams but nobody wanted it.

The Redskins also had me rooming on road trips with a coach, Floyd Peters. Talk about not trusting me. When you come to a new team, there's always a checking-out stage, but the Redskins were checking me out good, rooming me with the defensive line coach from the first trip on. It was like, We're gonna keep tabs on this cat right now.

It didn't make any difference to me because at the time I didn't really care whether I stayed or not. You don't like the way I act, trade me. But Floyd is a professional, and he respected me as a football player, and I respected him as a football player, so we just sat down and talked things out.

He said, "Look, you know why I'm your roommate, I know why I'm your roommate, so just play it cool for about two or three weeks. They're expecting something, so when it doesn't happen, they're just gonna forget about it. They're expecting me to keep an eye on you but I'm not going to sit down with a little pencil and paper and write down every little thing you do." We had an automatic rapport after that. We were both throwing our cards right on the table, and this is the type of person I like.

Floyd did have one drawback as a roommate, though. He was a sleepwalker. We were on a road trip once and he made some weird moan in the middle of the night that woke me up. I don't know what it was. I looked and he was just sitting straight up in bed, asleep. So I sat up, too, and watched him for a while, finally he just lay back down like nothing had happened.

I didn't get along with all the coaches, though, especially the two defensive geniuses, Sam Huff and Harland Svare. There are good coaches, and there are coaches, and then there was the Sam Huffs. He was the kind of guy who thinks, I was great, so I'm great now.

Alex Webster's a lot the same way. If you go in to talk with Alex you'll find out how many yards he made, all the honors he won and how great he was, you'll never find out what you went in there for. Sam believed all the stuff that was written about him, he believed it was him, and that was the way he came on.

Sam and Harland were like Pete and Repete. Whenever you saw Harland sneaking around, you knew Sam was one step behind him, sneaking around. He reminded me of a cat, and I don't particularly like cats. All of a sudden a door would kind of open very slowly, and then there would be Sam slithering around the corner trying to check out the whole room before he comes in. It must have been his New York Giant background.

I was in the dressing room before one game and Nate Fine, the team photographer, showed me a picture he took of me having my hands taped. I was showing it to the other players, joking about it, when Sam came by. I said, Hey, look at this Sam, this is great isn't it, pulling the string more than anything else. But he pointed to my mouth, which was naturally open at the time, and said "Yeah, look at that, that's the way you look to everybody." It's nice to be appreciated.

Sometimes I think I never left Sam's thoughts. Curt Knight, the team's field goal kicker, told me about one really bad practice he had, it was just one of those days when you just can't do anything right, and he was kind of shrugging his shoulders and feeling silly when Sam comes by and says, "Wipe that Steve Wright look off your face."

I got into trouble with Svare because I was constantly jerking around with the defensive line. It was a horseshit line, it gave up more rushing yardage than any other in the league. The team wasn't going anywhere anyhow, so I wasn't gonna beat my brains out against these guys in practice, I'd fool around a little. We'd run some plays and stuff, and I'd make signs like "touchdown," or I'd walk over and act like a referee and pull a flag out of my pocket and throw it down for somebody who was holding, or I'd wave my hands like, Go team, go. You had to do something to keep occupied out there.

Well, they took films of practice one day, and they didn't tell anybody about it. And not only was the defense getting eaten alive, to add insult to injury there I was, big as life, goofing around.

Svare showed the films to the defense, and he's saying, "Look at that clown, goddamn town clown, look at him, he's making fools out of you out there, you oughta kill him." After that, I found myself with the nickname of Bozo.

When I went out onto the practice field about three or four of the guys came up and they said, Hey, cool it, Svare is really pissed. Then Mike McCormack and Floyd Peters come over, and Mike says, "Oh,

133

incidentally, don't be messing around with the defensive players anymore." And Floyd, the defensive line coach, says, "Yeah, quit jerking around with my defensive men." And I said, Well, shoot, as soon as you get some defensive men over there that I can work against I'll quit jerking around with the shits you've got. McCormack just looked at me and shook his head.

The only other major run-in I had with Svare involved John Hoffman, one of the defensive ends, usually the meekest 6-7, 260-pounder you'd ever meet. During one practice, the field was really sloppy, mud and everything. We were working on the pass rush. John was the defensive man opposite me, and Svare was standing right behind him.

The ball was snapped and John came in and he just picked up a handful of mud and threw it in my face. I just stopped and stood there like, He really didn't do that. One of my idiosyncrasies is a rule I have, nobody hits me in the face. It probably reverts back to Alabama. It's degrading, it's like if you do that you have no respect for me as a man or a human being.

Svare was watching the whole thing and when John walked back to the huddle he said, "Way to go, John." Well, I was on Hoffman after that, I was taking out my frustrations toward Svare on him for the rest of the day.

After that, I forgot about it. I don't really know why he did it, maybe it was supposed to be a joke, maybe he just meant to hit me in the chest with it, or something. It wasn't so much that he did it but that Svare was standing back there condoning the whole bit, like, If you can't get him any other way, that's fine with me.

Svare didn't hit it off that well with Austin. Both were possibilities to succeed Lombardi, but Lombardi picked Austin. Though I have a world of respect for Bill as an offensive coach and as a man, his problem as head coach was that he expected professional athletes to be professionals, but with the Redskins he assumed too much. You just can't do it, because the team would take advantage, they'd cut your throat anytime they wanted, and this is what happened.

Austin is the kind of guy who's not gonna scream or yell at you. After bad games he essentially never said anything more than, Well, we lost. There were a lot of times we got the shit kicked out of us and nothing was said, or we just blew the game and nothing was said. Again, Bill expected us as football players to realize for ourselves when we'd made mistakes. If you're a professional nobody has to tell you when you screw up. But just because the Redskins got paid didn't make them professionals.

After one really bad day, we were all just sitting there like, What a horseshit game that was, and Bill comes in and his opening line was "Well, we got our fannies whacked." And I'm saying, We got our what whacked? You gotta be kidding, we got the shit beat out of us, we didn't get our fannies whacked. You're dealing with men, supposedly, and if I'm mad I'm not gonna say, Oh darn, I'm really upset. Bullshit. You've gotta say it just the way you feel it.

Bill's pep talks were kind of the same way, they weren't really pep talks, I don't really know what you'd call them, reminders maybe. They were just "All right, we've had three or four good days of practice, we've got everything down, we're gonna stick to the game plan, we know what we can do, what we're gonna do, how we're gonna do it, so let's go out and play football." Real inspirational.

I think the only time he ever departed from that was before our home game against Dallas. He made a comment just before we went on the field. I think he'd just ended his little talk, and he said "This'll be one time that the Indians beat the Cowboys," and that was it. That was his idea of a real zinger. Well, I mean you gotta give the guy credit for trying.

One morning I got in for practice real early and I'm walking through the locker room and I hear somebody say, "Boy, the longer I'm in football the more I drink." And I said, I'll drink to that. So who pops his head out, none other than Bill Austin. He says, "I knew it, I knew it, it had to be you."

Ideally, the leadership on the Redskins should have come from the quarterback, Sonny Jurgensen, maybe you've heard of him. But he just kind of blew on the spark every once in a while, gave it a quick puff. Sometimes it seemed like he had at least three personalities. I've seen him boisterous, but around the locker room, if he doesn't leave early, which he usually does, he's in a gray mood. Ninety percent of the time he's just blah, like, Well, let's get it over with. Nobody gives him any static because nobody gives a shit. Maybe he just doesn't trust anyone.

There was one practice near the end of the season when the team was out of the running, the coaches and everybody else didn't really know whether they'd have their jobs again, everything was up for grabs, the whole bit. So the coaches just told us to go out and work out on our own, do our calisthenics, then work up a sweat and "when you're through come on back in and we'll watch the films."

So after calisthenics Sonny ran back and forth for a bit and finally went to the dugout and sat down. And everybody else just kind of milled around, it was like a bunch of cattle, nobody knew what to do. And I said Hell, I worked up a sweat, I'm going in. I walked down to the dugout and Sonny was still sitting down there because he was through, too, and I said, Well, the hell with it, come on, let's go in. Sounds like a good idea to me, he says, not exactly what you'd expect to hear from a team leader.

Sonny did something even I've never seen before, he was drunk on the way to a game. I've seen people coming back drunk, but seeing it before a game really made an impression on me. It was the San Francisco game, the first of the season, and as soon as he came on the plane he was obviously drunk, really stoned. He's a readhead, light complexioned, so what happens when you drink? You just turn beet red, right? It wasn't from the sun, I'll tell you that. The rest of the team felt it was kind of amusing, like, Hey, here comes another one. I asked some of the guys and everyone said nobody ever drank on the plane when Vince was the coach. They wouldn't dare.

Nobody else really thought anything of it though, but it made an impression on me because I'd never seen it before. I never saw it to that degree again, but Sonny, like a lot of players, used to take a bottle of Scotch with him on road trips.

I got into trouble myself in a similar situation when I was in New York. We were given two beers coming back after a game, and I don't really care for beer, I'd much rather have Scotch and water, so I'd bring a flask of my own Scotch coming from a game. Well I got the word from Alex Webster that Wellington knew I was drinking Scotch, somebody told him, and he didn't like it and I'd better stop. I said, Hey, let that son of a bitch go out and play a football game sometime and come back and have a beer. What difference does it make whether I relax on beer or relax on Scotch?

With this type of nonsense, the Redskins were

strictly an up-for-the-moment type of team. As long as we were riding the crest of the wave, it was, Here we go, boy we're great, we're fantastic. We did beat the Lions and almost beat the Vikings, but it was like everybody trying their hardest to beat the Packers when they were the best, it was a one-shot deal. Because as soon as we came over that crest and started on the way down it was like, Oh, everything's lost, forget it, quick, give me a ladder.

There wasn't any team leader. The younger players didn't feel confident enough, and the older ones could give a shit less. There was no real spirit or spark at either end of the spectrum.

We ended the season at 6-8, and most of our games were real fiascoes. The two games with the Giants were probably the worst. I was looking forward to the first one, my return to New York, but that Sunday turned out to be a miserable rainy day; the field was sloppy, and I was mad because I was getting my shoes wet. I mean if you're gonna play and you get your shoes wet you don't mind, but just sitting on the sideline and slopping around in the mud, it's just terrible. Finally, Walter Rock broke a chinstrap or something and it was, Wright, get in there. The first thing that happened was my old Giant buddy Freddie Dryer gave me the big smile and I gave him the high sign. I got a standing ovation from three people—I'd given them all tickets.

The Redskins had a nineteen-point lead late in the

third quarter, but we ended up losing, 35-33. I could just see the team take a nose dive. It was the old, Well, we've got 'em beat attitude, let's sit back and watch the clock go 'round, and it went 'round and the score went up and all of a sudden they beat us.

After the game some of these guys went to their lockers and started slamming things around and crying and screaming, but I think that's all bullshit, I really do. Because if it wasn't bullshit, the logical thing would be for them to do something about it. If you're going to get that excited or that mad, well, then do something. But nobody did anything.

Another great game was with the Oakland Raiders. We lost that one, 34-20. It was one of those Monday night TV games, and up to then no team had won the Monday game after winning the previous Sunday. We had just beaten the Lions, and everybody was really shook. It was unbelievable, that big stink about Monday night TV games crushed the Washington Redskins, they couldn't handle it. It was like, We've never done it before and, It's got to be bad luck, we're on the West Coast, all kinds of little things. I kept thinking, You gotta be kidding me, it's just a football game. Go out and play football. It was just ridiculous, until we got into the game, and then it was horrendous.

John Didion was probably characteristic of the season as a whole. Poor John, that guy was so shook.

His one and only job was to hike the ball on punting downs, but he had built it up so in his own head that he couldn't do it, and all season he'd been snapping them over the punter's head. The coaches kept trying to get him to snap the ball, then look up. But first snap the ball, that's the main thing. And he'd go out there in practice and he'd snap and he'd snap and he'd snap and he'd snap. Right there, every time. But he'd get into a game and zingo, right through the uprights. No one else ever got the job, though, I guess they figured they were paying him, they might as well put him out there for something.

It got to be a joke on the sidelines, like what are the odds he'll mess up this time. And we kept trying to get Mike Bragg, the punter, to put six-inch cleats on his shoes to give him a better shot at the ball. During the Giant game in Washington, John was doing so badly the fans in the end zone stood up once to catch the ball when he hiked it. He managed not to screw that one up, and everyone on the team congratulated him like, Way to go. What more can you say? I think he went out the next time and messed up. John wanted to play football but I don't think he really had the feeling for the game. He just was not a football player, he didn't have enough of the tenacity or self-confidence you need to play, and he lost more every time he screwed up.

The highlight of the season had to be Larry Brown, after all he did lead the league in rushing. I don't think Larry knows how good he is. If he gained 1,000 yards he got 900 of them himself. They seem to over-work him, but he just wouldn't stop. He's going to kill himself, run himself right into the ground. He compares favorably to the great Green Bay runners like Jimmy Taylor or Paul Hornung because all you'd have to do is stalemate the defensive player and they'd be past you. If you beat your man then, heck, they'd get even more. If he was bigger or faster, he'd be just unreal. As it was he was a big improvement on the runners we had on the Giants. At New York you had to send an engraved invitation to the back if you wanted him to get to the line of scrimmage. You know, Come on I've got this guy here I want you to meet. If you can work it into your schedule, try and get up to the line sometime.

A highlight of a different sort was Leo Carroll, a defensive end. He was from California and he dug hard rock, so the team called him Woodstock. He bought a pair of leather pants when he went out to San Francisco and it was the highlight of the trip. The club was playing musical chairs with the defensive line for a while, moving this guy in and that guy out and the next week another person would be in there and nobody really knew anything. One day some coach tells him he's not playing more because he's got a bad image, a hippie image, in fact. So Leo went out and got his hair cut, and to show everyone he was really trying, he took to jumping rope right in the middle of the locker room. He wanted everybody to see, look at me work, here I go. It didn't do him much good, though, he was dropped before the end of the season.

I've been a loner on every team I've been with, this is basically my nature. The Redskins considered me a wacko, but they knew I could play football, and that's been the story of my life. When the team couldn't decide who would lead calisthenics on Thanksgiving Day someone yelled out, Who's gonna be the big turkey? It was the perfect opening for Bill Austin to yell "Wright, get out here." No one could believe the stuff I said to newsmen. Someone asked me about the girls in Washington and I said, The broads here are much harder, you have to play games, it's like Disneyland. Christ, you would have thought I'd sold out to the Russians. You're nuts, Wright, they'd say, How long you gonna be here? You must not like it around here if you say things like that. I said I didn't say anything, they asked me a question, I gave them an answer.

One of the problems I had was that I'm a Levis and shirt guy, I dig comfort. My daily outfit was my Army fatigue jacket and the whole bit, and when I'd walk into the locker room it was like, Haven't you got anything else to wear? And I'd say, Hey, I like you and we take showers together and everything like that, but I'm not going on a date with you, I'm not gonna marry you, what do you care what I look like?

I remember one time I was in New Jersey. I left about 4 A.M. Tuesday with this chick in a little Hertz Econoline Van. I drove all night, we didn't even stop to eat, and when I pulled into the practice field at 8:45 you could definitely tell that I hadn't been to sleep that night. We came out after practice and I walked over to my little rent-a-van and everybody's just standing there, staring. It's like, Why are you driving that? You're not supposed to be driving that. But as soon as they saw there was a chick in the truck you'd be surprised how many friends I had, and they all wanted to come over and see my new truck.

I think of the Redskins as a little Peyton Place. Everyone was nosey, they wanted to know what everybody else was doing but they didn't want to ask you.

As I think I said before, I don't dig going out to bars and getting it on with the guys. Hell, I dig chicks. I don't want to go out with five guys and drink beer at a bar all afternoon, that's just not my bag. So me and Roy Schmidt would mostly hang out at our apartment in Alexandria. We'd get our gallon of Gallo Burgundy and we'd turn the sounds on and have a good time.

Finally, Walter Rock, who has the locker next to mine, said, Hey, Where do you guys go at night? Home, I said. Nah, nah, I mean you know like when you want to go out and drink. At home. Nah, you know, if you want to go out and meet some broads or something, where do you go? At home. You're nuts.

I said, Hey Roy, come here and tell Walter what we do at night. What do you mean? Where do we go at night? Home. That was too much for Walter, he says Man, you guys are really weird.

I mean I've got everything I want at home, but they've got to find out "Where do you go" because there's nothing about you on the streets, we haven't heard a thing about you so I mean you gotta be doing something wrong, right?

In addition, the team sensed that it was going to be Austin's one and only year, so the whole general attitude became lackadaisical like, Well, this is a nothing type of thing, we're just marking time.

The week before the last game, Bill Austin made the announcement that if you wanted your last paycheck you could pick it up at the office the Friday before the game. And I'm sitting there with a big grin on my face and he says, "Wait a minute, Wright, we're holding yours until the Friday after the game."

He didn't have to worry though, because that game was the only one I started all year and I didn't want to miss it. It was against the St. Louis Cardinals, and I even gave a pep talk before it started. Usually only the two captains, Chris Hanburger and Len Hauss, made speeches. They'd get up and it was always the same stuff every week, like, This is a recording, This is a recording. Okay, guys, really go out and get 'em

145

now, Okay guys, really go out and get 'em now. Len would say, Okay Chris, you take it this week, and Chris would say Okay guys, let's go out and get 'em this week.

So I told Len, Look, I want to make a speech too, and he said okay. So he gets up and does his thing and Chris is doing his thing and I'm waving my arms, I wanna say something, I wanna say something. Finally Len says, "Steve wants to say something," and everybody goes, Aaah, no.

It was a nothing game, everyone kinda knew that the coaching staff was gone, including the coaching staff, so I got up and said, All right, we've been putzing around all week long, sitting around doing nothing. Nobody wants to play, I don't want to play, you don't want to play, even the guys on the other team don't want to play. But since we have to, we might as well win because I'm going goose-hunting tomorrow and I'd like to be in a good mood when I go. We won by a point, 28-27.

Really, it didn't make any difference to me at that stage of the season whether I got into a game or not. But I was gonna have fun, no matter what. Hell, if I'm gonna start one game of the year, I'm sure gonna have a good time while I'm out there.

I played opposite Rolf Krueger of the Cardinals, and we were just joking around the whole game. We got on the line once and I said, Forget it Rolf, it's going to the other side. The ball was snapped, I fired out and cut him down, and sure enough the play went to the other side.

Krueger just looked at me and said "Well I'll be a son of a bitch." And I said, Rolf, would I kid you?

CHICAGO . . . and AFTER

As a professional football player I've been traded five times, and when people ask me if that damages my ego, I say, Shoot no. I have a specific vocation or specialty that's usable somewhere, and where I can use it is where I want to use it. Besides, every time I get traded I get a raise, and that's the name of the game.

I didn't know I was going to be traded before the 1971 season, but I knew the Redskins were going to get rid of the whole coaching staff because Bill Austin's throat was being cut from the start. It was just a question of who would be hired to take his place, and it turned out to be George Allen, who came in from Los Angeles with all his money and his coaching staff and his players and everybody else to save the world.

The first time I met George was during a three-day training camp he called in April 1971 to set down the commandments of George Allen, to learn the new basic philosophies of how he interpreted football. Everything started off just about the same as usual for Steve Wright, because I loaned my car to a friend and my motorcycle didn't work, and I had to catch a cab to get there at all.

One thing I have to admit is that usually I like somebody or don't like him on first impressions, and I didn't like George Allen right off. I don't like somebody that's real soft-spoken and never looks you in the eye, and now I know my first impression was right. Because he'd try and sell snowballs to Eskimos, I'll tell you that. Even the day I was traded, he couldn't bring himself to look at me. I had to say, Spit it out, George. It doesn't bother me.

Some people say that Allen is supposed to have a rapport with the players, but the ones I knew that had played under him said that as long as you were a big name and could do something for George Allen, George Allen would do something for you. In other words, one hand washes the other. As for the rest of the players, they were just cattle in the herd, so to speak, and not too many of them trusted him.

150

In fact when you hear about how the Rams were going to fire Allen except that all the players stood up for him, it wasn't all the players, it was just the mainstays of the team. This ought to tell you something, because he never did much with the amount of talent that he had at Los Angeles. The Rams were consistently good, but with that type of talent you'd think they would have gone farther.

One thing I noticed about George even in that three-day camp is that he's on a constant reinforcement trip for his ego. For instance, he came up to me and said, "Don't you think this camp is really good, I mean this is really gonna help all of us, don't you think?" What can you say? Yeah, man, wow, I love to come out here for three days and work out twice a day. But he's constantly doing this, he loves to go up to players and ask them, "Well, what do you think about this, what do you think about this, isn't this good, this is great isn't it, don't you think it's gonna help everybody," and you're stupid to say, No man, it ain't worth a shit.

There's a feeling you have when you're not going to last with a team, you can really sense it. At the three-day thing I wasn't really sure, but as soon as regular camp started up in Carlisle, Pa., I knew it from the first. I was standing around so much I was getting out of shape at training camp. Allen would break everybody up into groups, his starting team over here and the rest of the flunkies go over there and circulate. I was always with the circulating flunkies.

Getting out of shape at camp got to me after a while, and I asked Mike McCormack, the offensive line coach, what was going on and he didn't know anything. In fact this was the whole thing with Allen, nobody knew anything but George, and everybody was afraid to do anything because it might not be what George wanted you to do. Delightful.

In every training camp I've ever been to, some guy comes up with a new idea that's going to revolutionize athletics, and 1971 was no different. This time it was a series of limbering-up-stretching exercises to encourage flexibility of movement and quickness. And actually, this was not a bad idea, but on the first day, with everyone . bending everything, I couldn't resist just flexing my little finger back and forth and saying: I don't want to overdo it too early. Believe me, I got noticed. I'm one of those people who can't hide, no matter what.

That was also the year we had a former Mr. Universe, Bruce Randall, come up as a strength coach. As big as he was and as strong as he was, he showed up in his black tights and freaked all the players out. Strength happens to be one of my bitches because I don't make my living with it, I make it with quickness and intelligence, 'cause there are a lot of big, strong people around that can't play football. But they had us go through a weight training program anyway, and I came out the weakest lineman on the team. Everybody was supposed to bench press his body weight, and I weighed 245. We started there and went down to 225, then to 200, and finally I barely pressed 175. Not very encouraging.

Eventually I was getting the idea I wasn't the Redskins' favorite player. Like when I showed up on picture day and nobody wanted my picture. I think George went around and told everyone "Hey look, forget Wright because he ain't gonna be here that long." So I went over by the fence, stretched out and enjoyed the sun.

What really sealed my fate with the Redskins was an automobile accident I had at camp where I ended up with a concussion, bruised kidneys and a messed-up back. I missed two of the exhibitions because of it, and when I was told I was going to play in the Baltimore game but didn't, that told me right there, it's coming, just hang on.

The problem was that as far as George was concerned I had put a black mark on the team and the profession of football forever, and that was it. When I got out of the hospital I went and talked to him and he wouldn't believe a thing I said. In essence George was calling me a liar to my face, and that got me mad. I just got up, threw my arms up, and went to Mike McCormack and said the hell with it, I'm gonna pack my bags, send me a letter when you know where you traded me, because I'm not going to sit around here just waiting for the time to come. Mike said "Well, you know, time heals all wounds" and stuff like that, but I'll tell you, it doesn't keep you from being traded.

So I went back upstairs and sat on it for about a week, went to practice and again it was the same stuff, I wasn't doing anything. So I went back down to George and said, Hey, make up your mind, either trade me or get rid of me or do something, because as far as I'm concerned you're jerking me around, and let's face it, if you're gonna jerk me around I'm gonna jerk you around. And his comment was, No, we wouldn't do anything like that without telling you. We want to do the right thing for you and well I've completely forgotten about that accident. I mean Christ, if he said that once he must've said it fifteen times, that he'd forgotten completely about it. He might have forgotten about the accident but he sure remembered that cliche.

By this time camp was about over. My roommate had been John Wilbur. We used to sit and rap and he'd try to get on top of me mentally and I'd sit there and laugh at him. But on the last day of camp we finally did something good. We had a party in our room, about 35 guys, everybody running up and down the halls screaming until about two o'clock in the morning. We even went in and woke up Billy Kilmer—as red as his face is, he sleeps early—and dumped him out of bed. Finally, just about the time everything had quieted down, when John and me were sweeping up the broken glass, up came A-Number One Flunky Joe Sullivan with this stupid grin on his face, saying "Well, what do you know, what's going on up here?" It was all part of the plan. Let the boys live it up on their last night.

When we got to Washington we found that Redskin Park was only half-finished so we spent most of our time practicing on a high school field and putting sticks into the grass to mark holes at the new park. Learning a trade, learning how to be groundskeepers for George. One day I rode my motorcycle out there and, just like in New York, that turned out to be my nemesis, because they told me I'd been traded to Chicago. The sportswriters wanted to know my reaction and I said I wished they hadn't waited until after wind sprints to tell me. And what would I miss most about Washington? "Central Liquor" I said, and didn't bat an eyelash.

One of the main reasons I got traded is that I didn't want to play on the special teams. Even under Bill Austin, I just didn't like them. On one kickoff I crashed into a photographer named Dick Darcey, rolled over and asked him if he had a cigarette. Another time I was playing up front and an onsides kick came squibbling to within maybe a yard and a half of me. I didn't want to touch the ball, so even though guys like Rusty Tillman were screaming at me to pick it up, I just stood there and watched it go

155

spinning past me. When we watched the films on Tuesday, sure enough you could see my head just following the ball as it crossed in front of me. And Austin turned the lights on and said all excited "Who is that? a lineman can pick up the ball, you can run with the ball, who is that?" I said it was me and he says, "Wright, you knew, you knew you could run with the ball." And I said, Yeah, but I don't get paid to run. And that was it.

Seriously, though, I have a psychological handicap against special teams because I have been hurt about three or four times on them and I can't see it. I told George I hadn't been in the league eight years to be on special teams. Most linemen are put in the wedge or have to break up the other team's wedge, and that's all right if you're a first, second, or third year man and trying to make the team, but I mean I was an offensive tackle, not a wedgebuster.

If you want to pinpoint it, it comes down to basic pride more than anything else. After you've played once, once you've been a starting player, you know the rest of it is all bullshit. For me just to play out the rest of my career on special teams, forget it, man. I thought I was as good as if not better than any of the tackles they had. I wasn't going to sit on the bench and just wait for punt teams or field goal teams or kickoff teams or something like that. I wanted to play football, period.

Looking back on it all, I still think George Allen is

unreal. He just boggles my mind. I can't knock the fact that he's won games and I'll have to give him credit for going with veterans and having a sound defensive football mind—he could care less about the offense, you know, give it to someone else. But how anybody can look up to the man or hold him in any kind of esteem, that I cannot understand.

George to me is a politician, a political coordinator. His greatest assets are his assistant coaches who have a good rapport with the players, which is why he hired them. As far as comparing him to Lombardi, it's like comparing a fish and a horse, they ain't the same kind of animal. George doesn't really know what it takes to make a good football player. He's too superficial, he couldn't motivate an amoeba. With Vince you hated his guts but you love him at the same time. George Allen, you just hate his guts. George motivates in one way and one way only, and that's money. It's known all over the league, George Allen pays money, and most of the good ballplayers you'll see having trouble have trouble over money. You can take the whole Washington Redskin football team and you might find maybe four or five percent—the young players who are new in the league—who'll give you a bunch of rah-rah stuff. But the rest of the team is going to say there's only one thing that makes them play as hard as they do and that's cold hard cash, period. Sure, a lot of them will put up with George's cheerleader bullshit. You know, you're right, George, let's sing Hail to the Redskins. As long as you're paying me $10,000 more than somebody else will, sure, you want me to say thank you, okay, thank you. You want me to say I like George Allen, I like George Allen. Just give me the money.

Another thing I didn't like is that George will lie to you to your face. That's nothing new, there almost isn't a coach around that hasn't lied or cheated or stolen something to get where he is, but I just don't like people who lie. Vince Lombardi, as far as I know, never lied to me. George Allen lied to me and kept lying to me and I knew it when I was talking to him. He told John Hoffman there was a place for him on the team for sure, there was no problem. So John up and moved his family to Washington from California, rented a house and everything else, and about three days later he was cut.

Sam Wyche is another good example. He screwed Sam, keeping him around as a taxi squad quarterback behind Jurgenson and Kilmer. Then Allen gets Joe Theismann and Sam might just as well pack it up. If he goes with another team it's going to be tough because he's never really had the game experience. Allen never intended to use him but I'll guarantee you he was telling Sam Wyche all along, Stick with George Allen, you're gonna make it. Uh-uh.

I've always maintained if a player's not going to make it at least you should have enough guts to tell the guy it's questionable, everything's kind of up in the air right now. What a lot of coaches do, including George Allen, is tell the guy, Don't worry about a thing, there's a place on the team. Like, Everybody's going to have a chance to do what they want to do, and all I care about is getting the team together and winning football games. That's all bullshit. All George Allen cares about is George Allen.

I flew to Chicago right after I was traded and took a cab to practice at Soldier Field. I kind of wandered around the stadium and finally found the locker room, put my bag down and walked on the field. Jim Dooley, the head coach, came over and said hello to me, and so did my Washington friend Bill Austin, who was now in charge of the Bears' offensive backs. And then Jim Ringo, the guy who would be my coach, came over and introduced himself, too. I wasn't supposed to do anything because you have to get checked out by the doctor first, so Dooley said just go on in, put on some shorts and come back out and loosen up.

As I was trotting around the field and looking things over, Jim Ringo calls me over. He starts right off saying, I know you've had a lot of trouble in the past with a lot of people but I don't think we're going to have any trouble here. Sure hope not, I was thinking to myself.

He says, I want you to know one thing. I know you're good friends with Bill Austin but if you need anything you come to me. I'm your coach. All I care about is you playing good football. I said I can dig that, that sounds reasonable.

He says, I want you to keep your nose clean, get your hair cut—it was a little long at the time—and stay away from dope. He says, I don't want you smoking that dope. I cracked up on that one. He says you do that and we'll get along all right. I'm saying to myself, Wow, man, this is a real beauty here.

I watched the rest of practice, learned the stance the Bears used, picked up a couple of plays, and that was about it. Practice ended and everybody started running sprints. Just then Ringo calls me over again. He says, Get in here and start running sprints.

I'm saying to myself, Now wait a minute, I'm not supposed to be doing that, but then I decided, well, no, I just got here, there's no sense in starting any trouble, so I ran a couple of sprints even though that's the worst thing you can do if you're not warmed up. Well, I thought for sure I was going to pull a hamstring, I could feel my legs tightening up. Luckily, I didn't.

That was on Thursday, and on Saturday the Bears were going to play in Houston. I saw the doctor and everything was all right and they told me they wanted me to play the second half against Houston. I was hardly what you'd call ready but they were desperate for a right tackle.

On the Friday we left for the game, I was walking

down a corridor in O'Hare Airport with Danny Pierce, who'd been in the same trade from Washington, when all of a sudden Ringo pops out of a bar and says, Wright, what do you think you're doing? I said, I'm going to the airplane. You know, what else would I be doing there? He says, You don't have a coat and tie on. Real sharp guy that Ringo, caught that right off.

I said we didn't have to at Washington. Nobody told us we had to. In fact, nobody's said much of anything to us around here. He looked at his watch like maybe we had time to go back to the hotel and change. Like there's twenty minutes before takeoff. You gotta be kidding me, I'm thinking. But, no, he wasn't kidding. I'm sure if there had been enough time he'd have sent us back. But there wasn't.

So Danny and I get on the plane and everybody's looking at us like, Look at those two weirdos, are they going to get in trouble. Like a bunch of kids in school, Let's watch the two new kids get in trouble. With that, Bobby Walston, the Bears' personnel director, comes back and says, Didn't you know you're supposed to have a sport coat on?

Like if I knew I would have worn one, but I just said I didn't know. Then I added, Nobody's said shit to us about anything. Which was true. You'd have thought Danny Pierce and I were lepers. The players didn't say anything. The coaches didn't say anything. You know, nice warm welcome from the Chicago Bears.

161

So with this Bobby Walston says, Okay, Shit, now are you satisfied? I said, Yeah, that makes me feel right at home. I felt like I belonged. Already I was beginning to perceive a team unity. The Bears were united by their misery.

After we got to Houston, I met my roommate, a rookie safety named Jerry Moore. We talked for a while and then decided to go downstairs for a sandwich at the coffee shop. When we got up to pay the check, there's Jim Ringo sitting up at the counter with a couple of other coaches. "Hey Wright, come over here," he says.

He says, "What time is it?" I looked at my watch and it was, say, 1:40. He turns to the other coach and says, "Let me see your itinerary." Then he looks up at me and says, "You got twenty minutes to get to your room, you better get there." I said, What are you talking about? Why was he sending me to my room? Was I a bad boy? "I just came down for a little lunch."

He says, "It's a $250 fine if you're not in your room for siesta." Siesta! It turned out the Bears have a two-hour siesta time every Saturday on the road when the players have to be in their rooms. Grown men going for a siesta! How can you take that seriously?

And speaking of fines, blink your eye at the wrong time in Chicago and you'll get fined. The Bears fine you for everything, I've never seen a club with fines like Chicago. You sit there and watch films and some-body says, "Okay, that move's gonna cost you $100," or "You didn't sit down on the bench, that's $200 for you." Every other sentence was, "That'll be $100 . . . that's $200."

Toward the end of the team meeting the night before the Houston game, Ringo asks me if I under-stand everything and I say, Yeah, but I'll tell you what, I'd like to see some game films. He asks me why and I tell him I've never played Houston, I have no idea about the guy I'm going to play against and it would really help if I could see some films.

He says, Look, don't worry about it. They're going to show up tomorrow and you're going to show up tomorrow. I'm thinking, Oh, terrific, I got a beauty here, man, a real piece of work.

Just about this time another assistant, Abe Gibron, yells out, Hey, Wright, we're putting you in the wedge, on the kickoff return team. "Yeah," Ringo says, "put him on that, put him on the kickoff team, we need some vicious people around here."

I'm thinking, Oh, Christ, here we go back to Alabama, another blood and guts coach, just what I need. I figured I might last another two days. I said to Ringo, I got news for you. If you're looking for vicious people, you got the wrong one. You want an offensive tackle or a special teams guy? Take your choice. You can't have both.

Dick Butkus couldn't quite understand my thinking

there. In his book, *Stop-Action,* he wrote, "That's really a different attitude. I could never bring myself to do it no matter how much I wanted to. I love being on the field. I'd play offense if they'd let me. I'd never come off if I really had my way.

"But Wright says he just wants to be an offensive tackle and doesn't want any part of those special teams. He said that something could happen that would put you out forever. He claimed he hurt his knee playing on the special teams when he was with the Packers and he'd never play on them again.

"Wright's made up his mind that no one is going to make him do something he doesn't want to do. He's going to lead his life the way he wants to and no one is going to change him."

I'll drink to that. We're totally different individuals, Butkus and me. I didn't get to know him at all until about halfway through the season. Late one Sunday night, after we got back from a road game, Dick and Ed O'Bradovich and a couple of other players and myself stopped by a bar. We closed the bar up, then picked up maybe a case of booze, went over to the Hyatt House, rented a room there, and stayed there all night drinking. That's when I really first met Dick Butkus.

I felt kind of sorry for him having to play in Chicago. He was as good as you're ever going to be at middle linebacker but Chicago just screwed him right into the ground as far as playing him when he shouldn't have been playing because of his injuries.

Dick was smart enough to know he shouldn't have been playing, but he went ahead and played anyway. Because one thing a lot of people think is, if you're hurt, you don't play. Well, that's bullshit. You get an awful lot of pressure from management and often as not you end up playing.

What you do is you take drugs to kill the pain, period. This is something that a lot of people don't know about football players, or are just coming to realize. If you hurt, you take something for it, and I ain't talking about Anacin.

I mean, if you have to have a shot or if you have to do anything else you do it. If you can't get it from a doctor, you go somewhere else to get it. Most professional athletes know drugs, which drugs they want, what the effects are, everything, and they know how much to take. Christ, it's your life.

Dick was really hurting and he played more than he should have. He just kept playing on guts and drugs probably. I don't know for a fact that he took them, but I know I did.

Like I say, management expects you to play. And I guess there's pride, or ego, involved, too. I think that carried Dick in recent years. Once you're on the field, you play.

But, in the back of his mind, I think he was concerned about the abuse his body had taken and the arthritic condition of his knee. It was really frustrating for him. His knee was killing him and he just couldn't do the things he used to. Hell, the pain was so bad it was killing him to walk, and that's ridiculous.

He didn't go around making a big thing of it, that wasn't his style. He was definitely a loner, but he was the team leader because of his performance, because he was a damn good football player and not because he was a nice guy or because everybody liked him.

He was kind of a towering figure. You wouldn't walk up to him in the locker room and say, Hey, wanna go out this afternoon for a couple of beers? He only had a couple of close friends on the team and they were mostly on the defensive team and that was it. He could have cared less for anybody on offense.

One of the guys he hung around with was Ed O'Bradovich. The only time Ed O'Bradovich ever talked to anybody on the team was if he wanted tickets from them. Then it was, Hey, buddy, come here, I want to talk to you, you know, you were his long lost cousin. But after that, don't ask him for anything.

Dick wasn't that way, but he was very tight-lipped, didn't say anything to anybody. The rest of the players accepted him for that because he was a hell of a football player, and that excuses his type of behavior. If he becomes friends with somebody, it's going to happen on his terms, it wouldn't be some extemperaneous thing that happens in the locker room.

Dick was probably forced into that attitude from the time he was at Illinois and was a good ballplayer there. Anybody who's in the limelight faces a certain insecurity of not knowing who his friends are. Butkus knew this. He was conscious of his status and also conscious of what was going on around him at all times. As far as all that backslapping and handshaking from the public, he would just as soon get up and walk away. An admirable trait.

It didn't take me long to find out it was true what everybody had been saying for years about George Halas, that he throws around nickles like they were manhole covers. I think six or seven starting players were playing out their options because they couldn't get any money. Halas runs the Bear organization the same way he did in 1921. He still hands out $250 bonuses like they were the greatest thing since peanut butter.

For example, there was this guy who was drafted by the Bears a few years ago. He came into town a couple of days before training camp started with just about everything he owned in a paper sack, and he goes in to see Halas about an advance on his salary. Halas asks him what he wants it for and the kid says, well, he's never been to Chicago before and he'd like to go out and see what it's like before he has to report to camp. So Halas says, "I think you're right," and he reaches in his pocket and gives the guy twelve bucks and says, "Here, go out and have a good time."

I'd been with the Bears about two weeks when I went in to see Bobby Walston about money. By that time I had moved into the starting lineup and it was definite I'd be staying there. But when I signed my contract, I was still with Washington, and when I moved to Chicago I had to pay rent for my apartment in Washington as well as the one in Chicago. Plus I had to rent a car because I had to leave mine behind.

So I asked Walston, very nicely, like you don't have to do it but I'm starting for you, I'm doing a good job, and I'd like a thousand dollars extra to pay for my apartment back in Washington. I didn't think that was asking too much. And it certainly would have made me happy.

Well, I got the expected Chicago Bears response. Walston told me, You have to think of the overall picture, what if everybody asked for a thousand dollars? I said, Hey, look, don't tell me about all these problems because I'm not concerned. If you care if I'm happy, fine. If you don't care if I'm happy, fine. But if you don't care if I'm happy, I don't care if you're happy. And that was it. I didn't get my thousand dollars.

In fact, this team was so cheap they made you buy your own rain jacket. It was pouring rain at practice one day and I was standing out there in a

T-shirt and shorts and somebody says, Don't you have a rain jacket? Well, go in and get one.

So I go in and asked the equipment manager for one and he says, "It's gonna cost you $10." I said, What! He says, "Ten dollars." I said, You gotta be kidding me. He says, "No." I said, Forget it. I walked back to my locker got out a big, camouflage-colored parka with a hood on it that I bought for duck hunting and used that.

Jim Dooley didn't mind my actions at all. In fact, he was quoted in the newspapers as saying I was playing real well and that I was a good relaxer for the team. I always got along fine with Dooley. My problems with the Bears involved management, which means Halases. The whole Bear organization is full of uncles, brothers-in-law, cousins, even sons-in-law. They've got as many vice presidents as a bank.

One of them was Ed McCaskey, Halas's son-in-law. One night we were on television together, a sports talk show, live, and I'm not sure he ever did get over it. He wouldn't speak to me for about two weeks afterward. I was asked questions like, did I think there was a gap between the management and the players? I had to think about that for, oh, maybe, a hundredth of a second. I said, sure, there's a gap because management's living in 1921 and this is 1971, and it went on like that.

Because the Bears were a lot like New York, the same bit, treat 'em like school boys. You've got to be careful of what you say, be careful of what you do, because there's always an eye looking over your shoulder. It could be one of George Halas's flunkies or it could be George Halas himself.

To give you an example: smoking. I smoke. Other players smoked. The coaches smoked. Everybody had an ashtray in his locker. If you've got an ashtray in your locker, it's there for a reason, right?

So a couple of weeks after I got there I was sitting in the locker room and this little old guy comes up to me. I knew who it was but I just acted ignorant. He says, "What have you got in your hand, kid?"

I looked at it and turned it upside down and I said, It's a Marlboro. Yeah, a Marlboro. He says, "No." I said, Yeah, it is, look, right here, it says Marlboro, M-A-R-L-B-O-R-O.

He says, "You can't do that. It's against the rules," I said, It's not in my contract that you can't smoke. He says, "It's a club rule." And, for like one split second, I wanted to look at him and say like, I'm 30 years old. Who the fuck are you telling me I can't smoke? But I decided, nope, I'd just gotten there, why mess it up after the first couple of weeks, so I turned and put my cigarette in the ashtray and George Halas walked out of the room. Then I went back and got another cigarette.

So the thing with the Bears was, it's okay to smoke, but if George Halas comes in hide your cigarette. It's okay to do this, but if George comes in stop

170

doing it. To me, if you're going to do something, do it; if you're not going to do it, don't do it.

That was how it was with Lombardi. The rules were set down, no ifs, ands or buts, and no in-between's. Whether I'm around or not, this is the rule. If you break it, you're going to get fined. Like Lombardi said about jumping out after curfew, I'm not gonna go out looking for you, but if you happen to sneak out and we run across each other, it's gonna cost you. There was none of the Mickey Mouse stuff, like, jeez, it was just a pacifier I had in my mouth, it wasn't really a cigarette, that type of shit.

To give you an idea of how Halas would try to instill esprit de corps in the team, that whole bit, the Bears one day brought in a Brink's truck with $25,000 in cash and stacked it up in front of us and say, okay, this is what we're gonna go for this year. Wow, man, look at that, five armed guards, the stack of money you'd get for winning the championship. You know, big deal.

Then there was W. Clement Stone, the millionaire friend of Halas, who was the single biggest contributor to the Nixon campaign in 1972. W. Clement would actually give us pep talks. That cracked me up.

I'll never forget it, we all walked in one day and the other guys were kind of snickering and laughing, they knew what was going on, but I didn't know what was coming. Butkus and Doug Buffone and Ross Brupbacher were kind of stretched out on the floor way in the back, the rest of us were sitting on benches.

This little guy, about five-foot-four with a little mustache, walks in with Halas, and Dooley introduces him as W. Clement Stone. He starts in like Billy Graham at a revival meeting and he's saying, "Every time I get up in the morning I say three things: I feel healthy, I feel happy, I feel terrific. Now, everybody stand up and say this."

And I'm looking around like, You gotta be shitting me, man, whoa, 9 o'clock in the morning and this dude is doing this to me. Everybody is looking around at everybody else and nobody's standing up. So with this Dooley gets up and says, All right, come on, everybody stand up.

Then Halas gets up and he says, "Come on, everybody stand up." Oh, shit, man. So everybody stands up. "Ready: I feel healthy. I feel happy. I feel terrific." Not once, but three times.

He showed up about four times that season, and every time he came, he would talk about how good he felt and how he had just seen the President and the President told him that he wouldn't be where he was today if it wasn't for him. And I'm thinking, Wow, that tells me something about Nixon, man.

One time he said, I want to make a prediction. I want to predict that the Chicago Bears are going to win by at least two touchdowns, and I've never been wrong. I think it was two weeks in a row he told us we were going to beat San Francisco by two touchdowns. Well, we went out there and got the shit beat out of us and he didn't show up for two months.

I initiated my own program for team morale that year. It was called LUPs, for Line Unity Party. Every Friday the whole offensive line used to get together after practice at a place called R. J. Grunts. They'd take care of the players there, all the beer was free. We'd sit around and bullshit, have a good time, talk over the problems of the team, what we were going to do that Sunday, and everything else.

Chicago was a good year for me because I was playing well and because I liked most of the guys. We got along great. I felt sorry for them because I know what football's supposed to be and Chicago wasn't it. There is a tightness on the Bears, but it's there only because everybody's pissed off at the same thing. Like I said, there's only one thing that holds the team together and that's misery. It won't change until Halas is off the scene and not even then because the Bears will still be run by the Halas family.

After a point, I didn't have any more trouble with Jim Ringo. I told him if I do the job on Sunday, play me, if I don't do the job get rid of me, but don't shit me. Not playing is a bummer but taking shit from a coach is worse.

The only other time I ever really got irritated

enough to say anything to him was once during a game when the offense wasn't going well. Every time the offense was screwing up, Ringo would just turn around and walk away when we came off the field. He would stand at the other end of the bench and wouldn't talk to any of the players.

I told him, Hey you, standing down here doesn't do the offensive line any good. You know, we're playing as well as we can, we're not doing it on purpose. I told him it was ridiculous for him to walk away because we needed somebody to get everything pulled together.

His point was that if the guys saw him turn and walk away it would make them so mad they'd go out and play harder, which might work in high school but not in the NFL. I had to laugh.

One other thing. We would watch offensive line films with Ringo and he would constantly use words in the wrong context. Like, if he was praising somebody he'd say, "That's a loquacious move." Or, "That's facetious, that's what that is." And another one was "cognizant." Like you had to be cognizant that that was a loquacious play.

The Bears had the only man I ever met who really scared me just sitting in the locker room before a game, and that was George Seals. He sat across from me and I could look right over at him. Wow, man, I've never seen anybody get that charged up.

He reminded me of a bull. You've seen a bull snort. George would get wild-eyed and sit there and go Snort, snort, snort, snort, and he'd tense up and start shaking physically. Snort, snort, snort, we'll kill 'em, we'll kill 'em. Wow. I'd walk over there and say, Jesus Christ, lighten up George, the game's not for 45 minutes, man. Shit, you're gonna scare me so much I won't be able to go on the field.

He was the same way on the field. He'd go crazy. He'd start screaming. Arghhhh, arghhhh, arghhhh.

You know, when he was with the Redskins they had him on offense, which shows you the ineptitude of a lot of the coaching around the league. It's a simple fact that offensive linemen have to be more disciplined and the defensive guys can go wild. And he is a wild man, no doubt about it.

I knew I liked George from the minute I got to Chicago. The first time I lined up in practice I was opposite Willie Holman, the defensive end. George was the defensive tackle, one man over. We didn't have helmets on and I'm thinning on top and my hair fell down when I bent over and he says, "Man, how old are you?" Then when I put my hand down to take the stance he took one look at my arm, and I don't have the biggest arms in the world, and he says, "Willie, look, we've got another weightlifter." Right then I knew George and me were gonna get along.

My first year at Chicago went surprisingly well. We won six of our first nine games. One of these turned into a nightmare, though. That was the game in Detroit when Chuck Hughes of the Lions died.

I think there were only about thirty or forty seconds left, something like that. It had been a good game. We were winning but it was close, 28-23, and they had the ball and were trying for a first down to keep it going. They called a pass play and Chuck Hughes ran down the field.

The play went somewhere else and Hughes started walking back toward the huddle. He got right about where our defensive huddle was and just fell down. At first, everybody thought he was faking to get an extra time out.

Then, all of a sudden, one guy ran out on the field and then he waved somebody else onto the field. Then you saw them carry oxygen bottles on. Then the stretcher. You saw them beating on his chest to start his heart again. Then they carried him off. And you knew he was dead.

Everybody was talking, saying Hughes was dead, and nobody wanted to finish that game. You didn't want to play but you had to. There was no cheering, no nothing. After the game, everybody just silently cleared out of the stadium. It was weird. It shook me up and it still does when I think about it. When you see it out there it brings it close and you know it could happen to anybody. That could have been me out there.

A couple of games after that we beat the Redskins,

16-15, when Butkus caught a 35-yard pass from Bobby Douglass on a screwed up extra point play. Then Curt Knight had a chance to win it for Washington with about a 50-yard field goal in the last few seconds.

Well, I've always maintained that if I'm not in the game, there's nothing I can do to change the outcome. Like in the last two minutes of a game with the defense out there and the score close, I'm not one to get up and jump up and down on the sidelines. I'm going to sit on the bench and I don't even want to see the game because I've done what I can. All I can do now is look at the scoreboard and watch those seconds tick away.

But this was one of the few times in my life that I was up on the sideline. It was the first game we had played with Washington since I'd been traded. I'd played a good game against Ron McDole, who's a damn good defensive end, and there was only one point difference. It was one of those few times I really felt like trying to do something.

"Odin, Odin," I started yelling to the Viking god of weather. "Odin, where are you now that we need you? Blow, you sonofabitch, blow." And George Allen swore after that game there was no wind at all until Knight's kick took off for the goal post and just then a gust came in off the lake and blew it off course.

The next day I was invited to the Quarterback Club luncheon. By the time I got there, there was no room for me at the speaker's table so I sat with the press. The players at the head table were introduced and everybody got up and said things like I love my coach, my coach loves me. You know, "Here's our next player, he's a great player. . . ." It was getting sickening. Finally, "last but not least, sitting down there at the press table, Steve Wright. Come on up, Steve, and say a few words."

I got up and really reassured everybody. I said, We have a very close organization here. In fact, we have showers together.

The Redskin game turned out to be the high point of the season. We lost our last five games and Dooley was fired. The offense couldn't do anything. We didn't score a touchdown in the next three games and only two the rest of the season.

What had happened was we had lost our first two quarterbacks, Jack Concannon and Kent Nix, because of injuries, and Bobby Douglass had taken over at quarterback. Well, Bobby Douglass ran the Redskins all over the field, but he just wasn't ready to play quarterback. He couldn't read defenses, had a hell of a time finding his receivers and he usually ended up running the ball. It got to the point where he'd just drop back, look once, couldn't find the receiver, and start to run.

One night Bobby Douglass took all the game films

178

home with him, parked his car near the Rush Street nightspots, and left the projector and films on the back seat. Needless to say the next day none of the films were there and neither was the projector. So for a week, we watched game films from two years before.

Which reminds me of a guard named Bob Newton. Obviously, he was known as Fig. Typical rookie. Lot of potential but could've cared less. He actually got lost twice when I was there. Literally. Didn't show up for two days. You know, came wandering into practice two days later, no wallet, no money, had no idea where he'd been. Nothing. Nobody'd heard from him. All of a sudden two days later he showed up.

When Douglass took over at quarterback, first thing I told him was, I took care of you, I got you playing because I got Concannon knocked out. Be good to me or you're next.

The problem was Douglass didn't know shit about how to quarterback the Bears because he'd never had to. He had been the third-string quarterback and he had nothing to do at practice so he stayed on Rush Street all night, roaming around, looking for action. You know, I'm Bobby Douglass of the Chicago Bears. That type of thing. Then, all of a sudden, there's nobody left but him and we had to adopt an entirely different method of football. He didn't know any of the plays and he never bothered to learn them. He couldn't even tell a 36 from a 37.

Dooley actually moved into Douglass's apartment, to keep him off the streets and make him learn the plays. During the game, Dooley would send in the plays via the tight ends. The funny thing was that the messengers weren't always reliable. I'd say they'd get things straight only about two per cent of the time. That's right, two per cent.

A lot of people think what's so hard about bringing in a play. Well, he's got to think of the play himself when the coach tells him, run on the field, tell it to the quarterback, then hear the play again in the huddle. You'd be surprised how hard it is with the tension of the moment and the crowd noise and all. And if the guy's not a regular, he's excited to begin with just being in there.

And another thing. Typical Chicago. Chicago's the only team in the league that won't say right or left. It's either north or south. And they won't say it's either a red or brown formation, which every other team uses. It's either a Mo or a Len. So, north Len 37, you gotta think, is this to the left or right?

So you'd be there in the huddle and the tight end would come running up, all excited, trying to remember the play, and mumble, mumble, mumble, he'd tell Douglass a play like south Mo split 39 and, invariably, the tight end would have come in with the wrong formation for the play or the right formation with the wrong play.

And Douglass would be crouched down there like,

180

"That's not right, that's not right," and the tight end would be saying, "Yeah, it is, yeah it is, that's what he told me to tell you," and the clock's ticking and everybody's there trying to figure it out.

So three or four times I called the play myself in those situations. Typical Steve Wright. Like for a lineman to call a play, that was unheard of. But, hell, it was better than getting a five-yard penalty for delay of game.

And we always made yardage.

My second year at Chicago started out like my second year in Washington, with a new head coach. Jim Dooley was gone, and Abe Gibron, who had been his chief defensive coordinator, was put in charge. There are two distinctive things about Abe. First he's a great big guy, about 325 pounds and about as tall as he is wide—he's supposed to be a fantastic cook, a gourmet chef—and second he was a screamer. All the Bears' coaches were screamers, like somebody robbed the First National Bank or something, but of all the screamers he's the best I've seen, you can almost hear him in silent movies.

The Bears had a three-day pre-training camp in April and I didn't fool around, I got thrown out the first day. The thing about these early camps is that they're not in our contract. We don't have to attend, but it's kind of, If you don't show up you're in trouble. And I found out later that they put everyone through two-a-day drills, just like in the summer, and damn near killed half of them, so I done good by getting thrown out.

Anyway, I'd flown into Chicago, checked into my hotel room, and as soon as I got my keys from the desk I see this big list of rules. You will be in at eleven, you will get up at six, you will have a coat and tie on at all times, you won't do this, you won't do that, all of this bullshit. And I'm saying, Wait a minute, you know, this isn't training camp. Football doesn't start for another three months, what is this? It just irritated me, so I stormed up to my room and found they'd stuck me with a rookie for a roommate. The first thing I did was unpack my bag, pull out a fifth of scotch and set it on the table. It was about 2:30 in the afternoon and we were scheduled for a so-called cocktail party at 5:30 that evening, so I figure, Well, that blows tonight. I was pissed off anyway from all those rules and regulations, so I said, Screw it, I'm going to the bar, where, naturally, I commenced to get blitzed.

Five-thirty rolled around and I pulled into the party, which consisted of coke or beer, not my idea of a cocktail party. But I was so blitzed by the time I got there I could've cared less. There was only one bartender behind the bar and all he was doing was popping tops on beer cans and cokes, but he still wasn't keeping with the flow, so I jumped behind the bar and started to help.

I'D RATHER BE WRIGHT

Well, I spotted a bottle of wine back there and since I'm not a real big beer drinker I poured myself a glass. I took it with me when we went into dinner, and when I finished it I got up, poured myself another one, and went back to my table. I was just sitting there having dinner, not being boisterous or anything, and Abe came over and said, "What've you got in the glass, Wright?" I said, I got wine. He says "Pack your bags and get out of here, I'm not gonna have that." I said, Dig it. And he says, "I'm serious." And I said, So am I. See you. I went upstairs, put my fifth of scotch back in the bag and caught a cab to the airport.

I came back to the Bears for regular training camp and got irritated all over again by all of Abe's rules. I think all that stuff is totally unnecessary. We're all professionals, we all have a job to do and it's ridiculous to start putting rules and regulations on us. For instance it was a $150 fine if you wore a T-shirt, a $150 fine if your hair stuck out beneath your helmet, if your sideburns came down below your earlobe, if your mustache came down below the side of your lip. You couldn't smoke anyplace but in your room, you couldn't wear a hat in any of the meeting rooms or the dining hall. All the coaches came in with their little coaching hats, right, but players couldn't wear a hat. I mean it just got ridiculous. I can't put up with shit like that. You know, leave me alone and let me play football, that's all I want to do.

A typical example of what it was like came right before the first exhibition game. We're sitting in the dining room having a pre-game meal and I lit a cigarette. Abe looks at me and says, Put that cigarette out. And I said, Jesus Christ Abe, look, we've got three or four hours before the game, and I want a cigarette. Where can I go to smoke? He says, Well, go out in the lobby. And here's the inconsistency of all of this bullshit: Everybody on the Chicago Bears team knows that I smoke, but what Abe wants to do is maintain this image that a football player doesn't smoke. So I can't smoke with my teammates, I've got to go out and sit in the lobby where everybody congregates and sees a football player smoking. I just can't accept this. You know, there's got to be a better answer than that.

What made the whole thing even more pathetic, really kind of a paradox, was that Abe had been a player and he knew how players feel about things like that. But players are really funny when they change that little status from player to coach. I think basically it's because they all thought at one time or another that they could have done better as athletes if they had worked harder or concentrated more. So when they make the transition, they decide they'll insure that their players give the maximum effort, but by hamstringing them with so many regulations and rules they defeat their own purpose.

Another rule we had was you couldn't go more

than fifteen miles away from camp. That was a $250 fine, but it still didn't prevent us from having some fun. I mean, you have to picture Rensselaer, Indiana. There's nothing there but corn. That's it.

So one afternoon three of us decided we had to do something and drove off down the road. Then somebody said, Hey, there's supposed to be a nudist camp over here and we all said, Let's go! So we stopped off at the first beer joint we could find, then headed over to Naked City.

We found a spot on the concrete next to the swimming pool, pulled up our case of beer, stretched out, and had a great time. Except for one one thing. We were out there from maybe noon 'til five o'clock and we were in agony for the next two weeks. Talk about a sunburn. When you have to go out and put a jock strap on and then your uniform and then fall on the ground and roll over, ouch.

Maybe Doug Buffone had a better idea. He simply refused to acknowledge the existence of Rensselaer. After practice, he'd just go to his room and stay in there and read books, He'd never come out of his room.

At the same time all this was going on, I was having salary problems, too. I had been the Bears' starting tackle the year before and before camp started they offered me only a thousand dollar raise. I said scrap that, I didn't even bother calling them back or anything. They contacted me again and gave me a bunch of stuff about I'm the highest paid lineman on the team and everything else. I said, Hey, that's not my problem, that's got nothing to do with me. I know what I want, and it's $5,000, period. Well, they said, we think you're being unreasonable. I said, Okay, but I was still your tackle last year all year long, I was one of the highest grading linemen you had, and I got the job done. That's all you care about, besides making money on Sunday. Well, I want to make some money, too. They said $5,000 was ridiculous and I told them, Okay, go get another tackle.

In fact they had drafted a guy named Alphonse Gaston, no, Lionel Antoine, who was the same thing as Alphonse and Gaston. It was touted he could play center, guard, tackle, tight end and everything else, you know, snap the ball, pass it and go out and catch it all at the same time. He was a typical big, cocky rookie from a little school who had to be the funniest man in the world because he thought he was the greatest thing since Band-aids. He was one of those guys who're always saying, "Who're you calling a rookie?" so I used to call him Super Rook. But he was touted to take my place at right tackle and they were going to move me to left tackle. And I just can't play left tackle, so forget that.

They still hadn't come up with another offer by the time we got to training camp, so I kept jerking around. My attitude went right down to the bottom, it was Okay, I don't care either. It got to the point

186

where Abe Gibron called me in to ask what was the matter, and I told him they just weren't going to pay me. He was the head coach but he had no idea at all what was going on, he was just a figurehead for the Halas organization.

The Bears finally did come up with some more money, a total of $3,000 I think, but by then I had gone through so much bullshit I'd made up my mind I was going to get what I wanted, period, or I'd just quit or get traded or go somewhere. Maybe if it had been a different situation where I was more at ease as far as the regulations and everything else, it might have been different. But with everything added together and rolled into a big ball I just said, Screw it, it's too much for me to hack, I don't need it and I don't want it. You get enough little things bothering you, it starts affecting the general reason why you're there. I was out there to play football, to play offensive right tackle, not to wear a coat and tie, not to have a nice trim haircut, not to put on an act like I was Jesus Christ Superstar. In the end all the little things built up so much that I just had had it, period.

I finally got traded about halfway through the exhibition season. I had a terrible game against Kansas City, my heart wasn't in it, my mind wasn't in it. I could've cared less, let Antoine play as far as I was concerned. Nothing was getting settled and I went into Abe's office and told him to forget it. I went back to my room and about ten minutes later one of the coaches came and told me Abe wanted to see me. I went down and he says, "Look, we just traded you and John Hoffman to St. Louis." I said, Okay, good enough, and as soon as me and John got back to our room we started going berserk, dancing around yelling, We're out, we're out. One of the coaches came in and just looked at us, like, Who are these guys, anyway?

One reason St. Louis had picked me up was that Bill Austin, who had gone from Washington to the Bears and was one of the reasons I ended up in Chicago, was now an assistant with the Cardinals. Bill was a guy who knew I could play football if I was left alone. But you start saddling me with all these bullshit things and I just get fed up with the whole rigamarole, everything.

The Cardinals were training at Lake Forest, Illinois, and the change from Chicago was just unreal, like going from Alcatraz to the Kahala Hilton in Hawaii. Everybody in camp was nice, the food was out of sight, the practice field and everything else was just great. They even rolled a keg of beer into the dining room once a week for a party. It seemed too good to last, and it was.

For one thing even though I got a raise in St. Louis, I had to pull teeth to get it from the Bidwell braintrust. Stormy Bidwell was a nice guy, but his brother Bill Bidwell, who bought the Cardinals, was a

188

real pip. He reminded me of the Little King, the little round guy in the comics who just sits there. He was always acting like, Well, I am Bill Bidwell. Well, big fucking deal, you know, that and thirty-five cents will get you your subway ride. I went around a couple of times with Bill and I finally took a thousand dollars less than I wanted, ending up with $34,000 my top salary as a professional.

As soon as I got to St. Louis I had my physical, which also turned out to be an unnerving experience. The team doctor started looking at me and feeling this joint and feeling that joint and saying, Well, there's a little crepitation here and there's a crepitation there. I was unfamiliar with the word, and the only thing I could figure out was "decrepitation." And I'm saying, Wow, man, this dude is standing here telling me I'm decrepit. So I said, What do you mean, crepitation, what is this, anyway? And he says it means there's noise in the joint. I mean every joint I got makes noise. And finally he looks at me and says, How long have you been playing football? I told him this was my ninth year and he says, You haven't taken very good care of yourself, have you? And I said, I'll tell you one thing, man, I felt good before I came down here to see you.

What really turned out to be strange, though, was that the Cardinals, a really close and tight-knit group at training camp, became, once they moved back to St. Louis, one of the most divided teams I've ever seen in my life, very close in fact to the New York Giants. There was no team spirit, period, no team unity at all. And I don't really know why either. You couldn't put your finger on it, which was weird. But I've never seen a team change so much from a training camp to their city as the St. Louis Cardinals.

Like you would walk into the locker room and nobody would say anything to you for fifteen, twenty minutes. Not hello, how are you, how've you been or how do you feel, nothing, forget it. It was the old players on that side, the new players on this side, and kind of a no-man's land in between. The one guy who dealt with that situation was a kid named Conrad Dobler. The young players were always making fun of him because he was a thinker, which is a bad thing to be in football. But he really wanted to play ball and finally he went out there and just beat the shit out of the people in front of him, got into like three fights a day in practice and he became their starting guard. Most of the guys, though, really didn't want to bother, they just said, Screw it, I'll play when I can and that's about it.

A lot of the trouble on the team was petty, petty bullshit. Like one of the things done by Dale Hackbart, who sometimes was the funniest guy on the team. This guy was unreal. He was a country boy and he could tell stories for three days straight, stuff like driving his car into his next door neighbor's living room, and never repeat one. Well one day, right before Thanksgiving, a big sign was posted in the locker room that some place in St. Louis was going to give each guy on the team a free turkey. You just had to sign your name, and the day before Thanksgiving you were supposed to go to some bar thirty miles out of town and pick yours up. I guess about half the team signed up and went out to that bar, but there weren't any turkeys to be had, Hackbart had had the sign painted up as a joke. This was the kind of thing the guys on the team did to each other. It's the day before Thanksgiving and half the team has no turkey, half of the team got screwed and the other half thought it was really funny. That's not the kind of thing that promotes team unity.

Another problem was deciding who was going to run the offense. We had permanent pick-a-quarterback week, it was like a quiz in the newspapers, who's gonna be the quarterback this week? We had Tim Van Galder, Gary Cuozzo and Jimmy Hart. Van Galder was all right for a while because he knew something, but nobody knew anything about him. He'd been around for a long time and he had a lot of ideas, but he'd never really played. His whole thing was just relax and do what you can do best. It worked fine for a couple of games and then all of a sudden he started getting more conservative with his play-calling, calling the same plays over and over again. People started picking up his pattern and he didn't do so well after that.

As for Cuozzo, he would go berserk at you for the least little thing, start screaming at the players and everything else. He could never figure out why something wouldn't work. "The play worked on the blackboard, why doesn't it work here?" one of those bits. Jimmy Hart was the most consistent, but I don't know, there's something about coming back to the huddle and seeing a quarterback just about ready to cry because he didn't get his pass completed. I don't know whether he was that way or not, but that's the way he looked to me.

I wasn't helping things too much at this point either, because St. Louis was undoubtedly my worst year in football. When I went there Ernie McMillen and Bob Reynolds were the starting offensive tackles, and since both had been there for years and both had been good ballplayers I'd adjusted my thinking to being on the bench and being a backup swing tackle. I was having trouble pass blocking anyway—the line coach at Chicago hadn't believed in it at all—and I was out of practice. All of a sudden Reynolds, the left tackle, was traded, and I knew what that meant. The kid was going in at left tackle, and I hate left tackle, I cannot play left tackle.

Basically, it comes down to three chipped vertebrae and a pinched nerve that affects my entire left side, so I have about half the strength in my left arm and hand as I do in my right. If I had been used to playing a little bit here, a little bit there, it might've been a different story, but I wasn't. I'd been exclusively a right tackle for eight years prior to that, my entire career, and surprisingly enough it's very hard to go from one side to another. All my movements and instincts were to one direction, to the right, and all of a sudden I'm playing left. For the first time in my life I really tried as hard as I could to be a left tackle, and I blew it. I stunk the field up in my own estimation, and that's what means most to me.

In other seasons, if I got beat clean against a good defensive end once, at the most twice in one season—I'm talking about without touching the guy at all—that was something and I'd never forget it. Shit, at St. Louis they were blowing by me so fast at left tackle I didn't even see their numbers. When we played Philadelphia, Mel Tom beat me bad, he was so quick, I mean I didn't even touch him. We were watching the films on Tuesday and Bill Austin says, Wright, you didn't even touch him. I said I know, but I called him a son of a bitch and I thought he'd turn around and say, What'd you say?

To make things just that much worse, I got hurt playing against the Redskins. We had a reverse called and I went to cut down Verlon Biggs and by accident he kicked me in the back and fractured four transverse processes. Those are the wings that stick out on your vertebrae, which is not too relevant except that all your muscles attach to them. I was out about three weeks, came back, played one game, pulled a groin muscle, and that put me out for the rest of the season. It wasn't, as I said, a particularly good year.

Not helping things too much either were the team doctors at St. Louis. They were under a lawsuit at the time so you got absolutely nothing as far as treatment except promoted natural healing, which meant, Here, rub some Ben-Gay on it and stick it in a whirlpool. That was it. If you got hurt, forget it, you couldn't get anything done because the doctors were so paranoid. In fact I told the doctor before one game, If we lose this one it's because we've got a bean gap, nobody's got any uppers. It got so bad that when we played the Bears I had to call them up to see if anybody had any uppers I could take.

There's been a lot of talk about uppers lately, and I've been in the league from the time you could reach into a big jar and take 'em, to when they were dispensed by doctors until there weren't any at all and I had to go out on the streets to get them. The main stink is always about abuse. We don't abuse them, we take drugs because we need them. I make my money for two hours on Sunday, and if I have to pop one, I'm gonna do it, no doubt about it. I mean we're not the normal everyday nine-to-fiver. I'm a person who has to go out there and if I have four fractured vertebrae I still have to practice or if I have a cracked rib I have to practice. And a couple of Anacin ain't gonna get it.

Drugs, and I can only speak for myself, are a tool.

They're part of my business. You're supposed to play. There's that funny, unwritten, unseen rule that you don't say, I'm hurt, and go sit on the bench unless you're really bad and you simply can't make it. If it's just to the point where there's a lot of pain, you take something for it and you go back on out.

My experience with drugs has been: They're there and I'm going to use them. You can give me all the arguments you want about whether it's mental or physical or what. I know this. I've been there with 'em. I've been there without 'em. And I definitely prefer being there with 'em.

The best analogy I can think of is this: In practice, I wear a shoe called a Riddell 45. They're just a little heavier than what Riddell calls its XP. Now you pick them both up and you might not be able to tell the difference in weight. But I feel quicker on Sunday with the XP's. If I wore the 45's, I would automatically feel like I was a half count slower.

Another thing about drugs, and I'm talking about uppers, if I can't get them from a doctor I'll get them from somebody else. I'll go out on the streets, you know, bars and places like that. In Washington, Georgetown was a place where they were available. A dollar a pill was the going price.

My favorite was a twenty milligram Biphetamine, or Black Beauty. I'd take at least one every Sunday. I never bought Black Beauties on the street though. They're capsules and they're too easy for somebody to take apart and slip some acid or something in there. So with those I stuck strictly with a doctor's prescription.

I'd take one about forty-five minutes before the game. Then, if I got hurt and my body was telling me to stop, I'd take another one at halftime along with a pain pill, usually Empirin codeine number four. I had them in my kit in the locker room.

White Crosses were popular, too. That's what they were called, a small pill with a white cross. They didn't do a whole lot for me so I didn't use them that much.

Daprisals were great for practice. Basically they're for periodic pain in women. They're great for practice because they're a muscle relaxant and they get you up just enough where you can keep going and you're not really tired.

Dexamyl and Dexedrine also were used. Sometimes I'd take Valium along with the pain killer. So on a bad game day I might have taken two Black Beauties, two Empirin codeine number fours, and a Valium.

At one time you could get all of these from the team doctors. They had a jar of Preludins—another upper—in the Green Bay dressing room. One of the guys said they're great for a game. So I jumped into 'em.

I had taken Preludins before, at Alabama, but not for a game. I was trying to get my weight down from 280 and some drug salesman at a hospital at Tuscaloosa introduced me to them. He had a shitpot full of samples. I was eating one piece of meat a day, maybe one piece every other day, and living on liquids. I lost 50 pounds in about two months but it almost did me in. I couldn't pick up a hundred pounds and put it over my head. But I never took drugs for a game before I got to the NFL.

Overall, the use of drugs in the NFL is very widespread. I'd say sixty per cent of the players use pills regularly and that would be a conservative estimate. Very conservative.

When I was in New York, things were tightening up to the extent that there weren't any jars but you could get a prescription fairly regularly from the team doctor. And that's usually what I did. I'd say I needed a prescription for twenty milligram Biphetamine, Empirin codeine number fours, Daprisals, and Doriden. I'd get a hundred of each and that would keep me for the season.

I took Doriden to help me get to sleep at night. It's a sedative. Basically I'm sort of an insomniac anyway and in the middle of the night things start going through my head. Just all of the bullshit that goes on in the NFL is enough to keep you up at night.

In Washington, you could get uppers the first year I was there. But it was getting a little tough. Like I couldn't get a hundred. I'd get maybe twenty of each. Then by the next year, just before I left, everything had been cut off. So I went on the street.

After I got traded to Chicago, I found the doctors there were fairly good. Again, not indiscriminate. But then the second year everything was cut out, period. And it was back on the street again.

I kept telling the doctors, look, if I freak out on the field it's because I couldn't get anything from you. It's going to happen to somebody sometime.

As I said, at St. Louis you couldn't get anything from the doctors. As far as I was concerned nothing much at all was going right.

All of this trouble put together was making me pretty disgruntled. I'd played a position I didn't want to play, I had the shit beaten out of me, I even got hurt. I mean this has got to sap your morale. I still went to practice every day, though. I couldn't do anything but I had to go out there and kind of stumble around the field. To make things worse I didn't care for the city of St. Louis either. There's nothing there—you could take that city and shove it off the edge of the earth and nobody'd miss it. I guess when you come right down to it I was just pissed off.

Fortunately, the girl I was dating at the time was a waitress at a bar called the Trap Room. I used to call it the Halfway House because it was halfway between my apartment and the practice field. And every day after practice they'd have a happy hour, doubles for a dollar and chicken wings to eat. I used to come in at about 6 o'clock, sit there all night long, and just get totally wiped out. Sometimes I think I damn near became an alcoholic in St. Louis. I just put away a whole lot of booze. After I was put on the injured move list I used to sit up in the stands, and I remember at the Giant game I was getting blitzed and some guy thought I was one of the other players. He kept calling me by somebody else's name and I kept getting drunker and saying, Yeah, right, that's me. I just didn't care.

I really only remember two players clearly from that year. One guy was Don Brumm, whose nickname was Boomer and who beat me out for the bad body award. He'd been in the league ten years and he loved beer. Don Brumm knew where every bar was next to every motel in every town that the team visited, and how long it took to get from the motel to the bar and back with a sixpack of beer. He could walk on or off a plane with six cans of beer under his coat. Don was my kind of ballplayer.

I also got reacquainted with Donny Anderson, who had been traded from Green Bay, and for the first time I saw him playing football and not just punting. He did real well and really surprised me. He'd gotten married, his attitude had changed a whole heck of a lot, and I think he had finally learned what football was about instead of playing the glamour boy. He really was a good ballplayer at St. Louis and tried to do some things to pull the team together, which changed my opinion of him a lot. It didn't work, though, nothing worked at St. Louis. As soon as the last game at Busch Stadium ended I got in my car and drove home to Washington, straight though. You better believe I was glad to get out.

After having such a bad season, I naturally thought about retiring, but I wanted to get ten years in for my pension. I'd had it with left tackle, I knew I wasn't going to play right tackle for St. Louis because Ernie McMillen's a damn good one, so I figured, Send me some place where I can play right tackle. They'd fired the staff at St. Louis, the whole bit, and when the new coach, Don Coryell, asked me what I wanted I said, Well, I want to be traded. He said, What's the matter and I told him I didn't play worth a dime last year at left tackle, I'm not going to take Ernie's spot at right tackle, so why don't you just trade me. He says, Any place in particular? I said, Yeah, how about Philadelphia? And sure enough, that's where they sent me.

I'd asked for Philadelphia because I'd heard that Mike McCormack had taken over the Eagles and I figured I'd give him a shot. He'd been the offensive line coach at Washington and his approach toward men, his honesty, reminded me more than anybody else of Vince. It's hard for me to put into words, it's just a feeling you have knowing Mike that he's not going to screw you and he's going to give you every bit of information that he can. All you have to do is go out and perform for him, that's all he asks of you, nothing else.

In fact, the most ironic thing about the Eagles was that they didn't know how to take good coaches like Mike. They couldn't believe it. It was like, This really isn't happening, they gotta be kidding us. A number of players, guys like Gary Pettigrew and Mel Tom and others, told me stories of coaches actually telling players on the practice field, Don't ask me questions because you get me confused. Other coaches wouldn't answer any questions, period. They had good ballplayers, good potential, but they just didn't know how to accept a good coaching staff. They really couldn't believe what was going on, that the coaches actually knew as much as they did and would give them all the help they wanted. They just weren't used to it.

When I got to the Eagles' camp at Chester, Pennsylvania, I said to Mike, If I can play for you, fine, but I will not play left tackle, and he says, Well, I'll tell you what, after watching the films I don't think you can. And I agreed with him. Mike put me at right tackle, but even there I wasn't doing well at all. I don't know whether I wasn't in shape or whether playing left tackle had screwed me up, but I wasn't worth a dime. I like to think that with a little bit of time I would have gotten it back, but I knew I wasn't pass blocking the way I could. And for the first time in my life I got into one of those situations where in the back of my mind I was wondering if I had maybe gotten a count slower, and should I really still be playing. Mentally, my head wasn't there anymore. I was on my way out. I knew it, Mike knew it, the whole bit.

I didn't get into the first exhibition game against Buffalo and so I knew right there like forget it. And two or three days later Mike called me into his office. They had five offensive tackles, and this rookie Jerry Sizemore really looked good, and Mike says, Look, we just don't need you, what do you want me to do? I said, Nothing, forget it. Well, he says, do you want me to trade you someplace or put you on waivers or what? I said, Nope, I've had it, see you. Basically, I'd wanted to play for Mike, period. That was going to be my last year anyway and if I couldn't play for him, I'd been too many places and seen too many things and I just was fed up with it. Plus I had this, Was I a count slow type thing, and within myself I knew for a fact that I was done. It just wasn't there anymore. I got a letter a week or two later releasing me from my contract, and that was it.

Only one thing bothered me about leaving professional football, and it was that I wasn't able to go out the way I wanted to, and I don't mean playing for the Dolphins or winning the Super Bowl or anything like that. It was something I couldn't have done with Mike, I liked him too much for that. But with a team like St. Louis or Chicago or New York it would have been perfect. I wanted to wait until about the third quarter of the last game of the season, move my hand before the ball was snapped and get a five yard penalty for illegal motion. Then I planned to get up, turn around, take my helmet off, throw it down and just walk off the field, leaving a piece of equipment every two or three yards. That's what I really wanted to do, and believe me, I would have done it, too.

When I got back to Washington after the Eagles camp, I did nothing for a couple of days and then started bartending, but that got depressing. I really can't see getting into a straight job, with everybody crawling over everybody else. Every time I drive past the Pentagon and see all those cars sitting there, nothing but a solid stream of cars, it reminds me of ants heading into the big ant hill. I've been in enough cities and I just can't hack them.

Not playing football, I can feel myself changing, and I'm as happy as I can be. I'm losing weight because I don't have to maintain it anymore, and my attitude towards so many different things is changing, too. I've been putting up with bullshit all my life— "You've got to do this, you can't do this unless you do this, you can't be a football player unless you do this"—and I'm fed up with all of it. My whole life has been one big mold, and I don't need it anymore, it's my past. I'm a firm believer that life is nothing but a series of beginnings and endings. I've ended one cycle in my life and I'm starting a new one.

Right now there's a lot of dental work I've been

putting off for five years—no sense getting them fixed, they'd just get knocked out again—that I've got to get done, and I've been working on the back end of my truck. It's a three-quarter-ton, four-wheel drive pickup with a camper on the back, and when everything's ready I'm just gonna take off, just go somewhere as far back as I can go and live. I'm thinking about going up the Alcan Highway to Alaska, seeing a road and just heading on down it, fishing and hunting and kind of living off the land. I'm just fed up with all the bullshit that's going on now, and whether I freeze to death in Alaska or Canada or do something else, I know I won't change myself to get ahead or acquiesce to someone else's demands. Because once I've done that, Steve Wright no longer exists. And that ain't gonna happen.

EPILOGUE

Even 6-foot-6, 250-pound football players can't arrange life the way they want it, and Steve Wright's first year out of the National Football League did not end up quite as he had envisioned. The energy crisis and its shortage of gasoline made his planned rambles through the wilds in a gas-eating camper impossible, and at the same time a new professional group, the World Football League, was formed. The league made Steve an offer and, ever pragmatic, he accepted and signed a three-year contract with the Chicago Fire. The beat goes on.